MW00988630

NEVER GIVE UP

Also by Max Lucado

Inspirational

3:16
A Gentle Thunder
A Love Worth Giving
And the Angels Were Silent
Anxious for Nothing
Because of Bethlehem
Before Amen
Come Thirsty
Cure for the Common Life
Facing Your Giants
Fearless
Glory Days
God Came Near
God Never Gives Up on You
Grace
Great Day Every Day
He Chose the Nails
He Still Moves Stones
Help Is Here
How Happiness Happens
In the Eye of the Storm
In the Grip of Grace
It's Not About Me
Just Like Jesus
Max on Life
More to Your Story
Next Door Savior
No Wonder They Call
Him the Savior
On the Anvil
Outlive Your Life
Six Hours One Friday
The Applause of Heaven
The Great House of God
Traveling Light
Unshakable Hope
What Happens Next
When Christ Comes
When God Whispers
Your Name

You Are Never Alone
You'll Get Through This
You Were Made for
This Moment

Compilations

Begin Again
In the Footsteps of the Savior
Jesus
Start with Prayer
They Walked with God

Fiction

Christmas Stories
Miracle at the Higher
Grounds Café
The Christmas Candle

Bibles (General Editor)

The Lucado Encouraging
Word Bible
Children's Daily
Devotional Bible
Grace for the Moment
Daily Bible
The Lucado Life
Lessons Study Bible

Children's Books

A Max Lucado
Children's Treasury
Bedtime Prayers
for Little Ones
God Always Keeps
His Promises
God Forgives Me, and
I Forgive You
Grace for the Moment:
365 Devotions for Kids
Hermie, a Common
Caterpillar
I'm Not a Scaredy Cat
Itsy Bitsy Christmas
Just in Case You Ever Wonder
Just in Case You
Ever Feel Alone
Lucado Treasury of
Bedtime Prayers

One Hand, Two Hands
Thank You, God,
for Blessing Me
Thank You, God,
for Loving Me
The Crippled Lamb
The Oak Inside the Acorn
You Are Special
Where'd My Giggle Go?

Young Adult Books

3:16
It's Not About Me
Make Every Day Count
Wild Grace
You Were Made to
Make a Difference
Anxious for Nothing
(Young Readers Edition)
One God, One Plan, One Life
Unshakable Hope
Promise Book
You Can Count on God

Gift Books

Calm Moments for
Anxious Days
Fear Not Promise Book
God Is with You Every Day
God Thinks You're Wonderful
God Will Help You
Grace for the Moment
Grace for the Moment
Family Devotional
Grace for the Moment
for Moms
Grace Happens Here
Happy Today
Let the Journey Begin
Live Loved
Praying the Promises
Safe in the Shepherd's Arms
Trade Your Cares for Calm
You Can Count on God

Max Lucado

NEVER GIVE UP

GOD IS
GOOD
WHEN LIFE
ISN'T

THOMAS NELSON
Since 1798

ISBN 978-1-4003-4899-2 (HC)
ISBN 978-1-4003-4898-5 (audiobook)
ISBN 978-1-4003-4897-8 (ePub)

Library of Congress Cataloging-in-Publication Data

978-1-4003-4899-2

Printed in the United States of America

25 26 27 28 29 LBC 5 4 3 2 1

CONTENTS

ONE

DOWN IN A HOLE

The boy's body slammed against the pit's clammy walls as he plummeted down, down the dank hole to the bottom. He landed with a thump, his aching head bobbing like a rag doll's. Yet the wounds of his body were overrun by the unimaginable reality of betrayal. Rejection. Hopelessness.

> So it came to pass, when Joseph had come to his brothers, that they stripped Joseph of his tunic, the tunic of many colors that was on him. Then they took him and cast him into a pit. And the pit was empty; there was no water in it.
>
> And they sat down to eat a meal. (Gen. 37:23–25)

He was in an abandoned cistern, jagged rocks and roots extending from its sides. A seventeen-year-old boy alone at the bottom. Downy beard, spindly arms and legs. His hands were bound, ankles tied. He lay on his side, knees to chest, cramped in the small space. The sand was wet with spittle, where he had drooled. His eyes were wide with fear. His voice was hoarse from screaming. It wasn't that his brothers didn't hear him. Twenty-two years later, when a famine had tamed their swagger and guilt had dampened their pride, they would confess, "We saw the anguish of his soul when he pleaded with us, and we would not hear" (Gen. 42:21).

These are the great-grandsons of Abraham. The sons of Jacob. Couriers of God's covenant to a galaxy of people. Tribes will bear their banners. The name of Jesus Christ will appear on their family tree. They are the Scriptures' equivalent of royalty. Yet on this day they were the Bronze Age version of a dysfunctional family. They could have had their own reality TV show. In the shadow of a sycamore, in earshot of Joseph's appeals, they chewed on venison and passed the wineskin. Cruel and oafish. Hearts as hard as the Canaanite desert. Lunch mattered more than their brother. They despised the boy. "They hated him and could not speak peaceably to him. . . . They hated him even more. . . . They hated him. . . . His brothers envied him" (37:4–11).

Here's why. Their father pampered Joseph like a

prized calf. Jacob had two wives, Leah and Rachel, but one love—Rachel. When Rachel died, Jacob kept her memory alive by fawning over their first son. The brothers worked all day. Joseph played all day. They wore clothes from a secondhand store. Jacob gave Joseph a hand-stitched, multicolored cloak with embroidered sleeves. They slept in the bunkhouse. He had a queen-sized bed in his own room. While they ran the family herd, Joseph, Daddy's little darling, stayed home. Jacob treated the eleventh-born like a firstborn. The brothers spat at the sight of Joseph.

To say the family was in crisis would be like saying a grass hut might be unstable in a hurricane.

The brothers caught Joseph far from home, sixty miles away from Daddy's protection, and went nuclear on him. "They *stripped* Joseph of his tunic. . . . They *took* him and *cast* him into a pit" (Gen. 37:23–24). Defiant verbs. They wanted not only to kill Joseph but also hide his body. This was a murderous cover-up from the get-go. "We shall say, 'Some wild beast has devoured him'" (37:20).

Joseph didn't see this assault coming. He didn't climb out of bed that morning and think, *I'd better dress in padded clothing because this is the day I get tossed into a hole*. The attack caught him off guard.

3

So did yours. Joseph's pit came in the form of a cistern. Maybe yours came in the form of a diagnosis, a foster home, or a traumatic injury. Joseph was thrown in a hole and despised. And you? Thrown in an unemployment line and forgotten. Thrown into a divorce and abandoned. Into a bed and abused. The pit. A kind of death, waterless and austere. Some people never recover. Life is reduced to one quest: Get out and never be hurt again.

Easier said than done. Pits have no easy exits.

Joseph's story got worse before it got better. Abandonment led to enslavement, then entrapment, and finally imprisonment. He was sucker punched. Sold out. Mistreated. People made promises only to break them, offered gifts only to take them back. If hurt were a swampland, then Joseph was sentenced to a life of hard labor in the Everglades.

Yet he never gave up. Bitterness never staked its claim. Anger never metastasized into hatred. His heart never hardened; his resolve never vanished. He not only survived; he thrived. He ascended like a helium balloon. An Egyptian official promoted him to chief servant. The prison warden placed him over the inmates. And Pharaoh, the highest ruler on the planet, shoulder-tapped Joseph to serve as his prime minister. By the end of his life, Joseph was the second-most powerful man of his generation. It is not hyperbole to state that he saved the world from starvation. How would that look on a résumé?

JOSEPH
Son of Jacob
Graduated with honors from the
University of Hard Knocks
Director of Global Effort to Save Humanity
Succeeded

How? How did he flourish in the midst of tragedy? We don't have to speculate. Some twenty years later the roles were reversed, Joseph as the strong one and his brothers the weak ones. They came to him in dread. They feared he would settle the score and throw them into a pit of his own making. But Joseph didn't. And in his explanation, we find his inspiration.

> As for you, you meant evil against me, but God meant
> it for good in order to bring about this present result,
> to preserve many people alive. (Gen. 50:20 NASB)

In God's hands, intended evil becomes eventual good—which is why we should never give up.

Joseph never gave up. He tied himself to the pillar of this promise and held on for dear life. Nothing in his story glosses over the *presence* of evil. Quite the contrary. Bloodstains and tearstains are everywhere. Joseph's heart was rubbed raw against the rocks of disloyalty and miscarried justice. Yet time and time again God redeemed the pain. The torn robe became a royal one. The pit became a palace. The broken family grew old together. The very acts intended to destroy God's servant turned out to strengthen him.

> In God's hands, intended evil becomes eventual good— which is why we should never give up.

"You *meant* evil against me," Joseph told his brothers, using a Hebrew verb that traces its meaning to "weave" or "plait."[1] "You *wove* evil," he was saying, "but God *rewove* it together for good."

God, the Master Weaver. He stretches the yarn and intertwines the colors, the ragged twine with the velvet strings, the pains with the pleasures. Nothing escapes his reach. Every king, despot, weather pattern, and molecule is at his command. He passes the shuttle back and forth across the generations, and as he does, a design emerges. Satan weaves; God reweaves.

By giving us stories like Joseph's, God allows us to study his plans. Such disarray! Brothers dumping brother. Entitlements. Famines and family feuds scattered about like nails and cement bags on a vacant lot. Satan's logic was sinister and simple: Destroy the family of Abraham and thereby destroy his seed, Jesus Christ. All of hell, it seems, set its target on Jacob's boys.

Satan weaves; God reweaves.

But watch the Master Weaver at work. He zigged when the enemy zagged. Created a pattern. Blended the pain into a palette until the chaos of Genesis 37:24 ("They . . . cast him into a pit") became the triumph of "life for many people" (Gen. 50:20 MSG).

God redeemed the story of Joseph. Can't he redeem your story as well?

Perhaps that's tough to hear in the midst of your pain. But God never changes. Our Father is good even when life isn't. If you're in the bottom of a pit, let me urge you: Don't give up. And though it's hard to imagine during the heaviest storms—*you'll get through this.*

You fear you won't. We all do. We fear the depression will never lift, the yelling will never stop, the pain will never leave. Here in the pits, surrounded by steep walls and angry brothers, we wonder, *Will this gray sky ever brighten? This load ever lighten?* We feel stuck, trapped, locked in. Predestined for failure. Will we ever exit this pit?

Our Father is good even when life isn't.

Yes! Deliverance is to the Bible what jazz music is to Mardi Gras: bold, brassy, and everywhere.

Out of the lions' den for Daniel, the prison for Peter, the whale's belly for Jonah, Goliath's shadow for David, the storm for the disciples, disease for the lepers, doubt for Thomas, the grave for Lazarus, and the shackles for Paul. God gets us through stuff. *Through* the Red Sea onto dry ground (Ex. 14:22), *through* the wilderness (Deut. 29:5), *through* the valley of the shadow of death (Ps. 23:4), and *through* the deep sea (Ps. 77:19).

Through is a favorite word of God's:

> When you pass *through* the waters, I will be
> with you;
> And *through* the rivers, they shall not
> overflow you.
> When you walk *through* the fire, you shall not
> be burned,
> Nor shall the flame scorch you. (Isa. 43:2)

It won't be painless. Have you wept your final tear or received your last round of chemotherapy? Not necessarily. Will your unhappy marriage become happy in a heartbeat? Not likely. Are you exempt from any trip to the cemetery? Does God guarantee the absence of struggle and the abundance of strength? Not in this life. But he does pledge to reweave your pain for a higher purpose.

It won't be quick. Joseph was seventeen years old when his brothers abandoned him. He was at least thirty-seven when he saw them again. Another couple of years passed before he saw his father.[2] Sometimes God takes his time: One hundred twenty years to prepare Noah for the flood, eighty years to prepare Moses for his work. God called young David to be king but returned him to the sheep pasture. He called Paul to be an apostle and then isolated him in Arabia for perhaps three years. Jesus was on the earth for three decades before he built anything more than a kitchen table.

How long will God take with you? He may take his time. His history is redeemed not in minutes but in lifetimes.

But God will use your mess for good. We see a perfect mess; God sees a perfect chance to train, test, and teach the future prime minister. We see a prison; God sees a kiln. We see famine; God sees the relocation of his chosen lineage. We call it Egypt; God calls it protective custody, where the sons of Jacob can escape barbaric Canaan and multiply abundantly in peace. We see Satan's tricks and ploys. God sees Satan tripped and foiled.

We see
Satan's tricks
and ploys.
God sees
Satan tripped
and foiled.

Let me be clear. You are a version of Joseph in your generation. You represent a challenge to Satan's plan. You carry something of God within you, something noble and holy, something the world needs—wisdom, kindness, mercy, skill. If Satan can neutralize you, he can mute your influence.

The story of Joseph is in the Bible for this reason: to teach you to trust God to trump evil. What Satan intends for evil, God the Master Weaver redeems for good.

Joseph would be the first to tell you that life in the pit stinks. Yet for all its rottenness doesn't the pit do this much? It forces you to look upward. Someone from *up there* must come *down here* and give you a hand. God did for Joseph. At the right time, in the right way, he will do the same for you.

— REFLECTION QUESTIONS —

1. Have you stood at the bedside of a dying family member or friend? Describe that moment and how it affected your faith.

2. Think of a moment from your past that was difficult to handle. A tough spot. How did people attempt to comfort you or advise you during that season?

3. Read through Genesis 37 to gain some background information about Joseph's family and the origins of his story. What are some red flags from verses 1–11 that foreshadow what happened in verses 12–36?

4. Joseph kept being thrown "down" throughout the second half of this chapter. Down to the pit. Down to Egypt. Down to the auction block. How do you typically handle the "downs" of life?

5. How would you *like* to handle the downs of life? Meaning, if you could choose the right response ahead of time, what would it be? What would that look like?

6. Here is a core promise from this chapter: *In God's hands, intended evil becomes eventual good.* When have you experienced that reality in your story?

TWO

DOWN TO EGYPT

Joseph's troubles started when his mouth did. He came to breakfast one morning, bubbling and blabbing in sickening detail about the images he had seen in his sleep: sheaves of wheat lying in a circle, all bundled up, ready for harvest. Each one tagged with the name of a different brother—Reuben, Gad, Levi, Zebulun, Judah. . . . Right in the center of the circle was Joseph's sheaf. In his dream only his sheaf stood up. The implication: You will bow down to me.

Did he expect his brothers to be excited about this? To pat him on the back and proclaim, "We will gladly kneel before you, our dear baby brother"? They didn't. They kicked dust in his face and told him to get lost.

He didn't take the hint. He came back with another dream. Instead of sheaves it was now stars, a sun, and

13

a moon. The stars represented the brothers. The sun and moon symbolized Joseph's father and deceased mother. All were bowing to Joseph. *Joseph!* The kid with the elegant coat and soft skin. They, bow down to him?

He should have kept his dreams to himself.

Perhaps Joseph was thinking that very thing as he sat in the bottom of that cistern. His calls for help hadn't done any good. His brothers had grabbed the chance to seize and silence him once and for all.

But from deep in the pit, Joseph detected a new sound—the sound of a wagon and a camel, maybe two. Then a new set of voices. Foreign. They spoke to the brothers with an accent. Joseph strained to understand the conversation.

"We'll sell him to you . . ."

"How much?"

"Trade for your camels . . ."

Joseph looked up to see a circle of faces staring down at him.

Finally one of the brothers was lowered into the pit on the end of a rope. He wrapped both arms around Joseph, and the others pulled them out.

The traders examined Joseph from head to toe. They stuck fingers in his mouth and counted his teeth. They pinched his arms for muscle. The brothers made their pitch: "Not an ounce of fat on those bones. Strong as an ox. He can work all day."

The merchants huddled, and when they came back with an offer, Joseph realized what was happening. "Stop this! Stop this right now! I am your brother! You can't sell me!" His brothers shoved him to the side and began to barter.

"What will you pay for him?"

"We'll give you ten coins."

"No less than thirty."

"Fifteen and no more."

"Twenty-five."

"Twenty, and that is our last offer."

The brothers took the coins, grabbed the fancy coat, and walked away. Joseph fell on his knees and wailed. The merchants tied one end of a rope around his neck and the other to the wagon. Joseph, dirty and tear-stained, had no choice but to follow. He fell in behind the creaking wagon and the rack-ribbed camels. He cast one final glance over his shoulder at the backs of his brothers, who disappeared over the horizon.

"Help me!"

No one turned around.

"His brothers . . . sold him for twenty pieces of silver

to the Ishmaelites who took Joseph with them down to Egypt" (Gen. 37:28 MSG).

Just a few hours ago Joseph's life was looking up. He had a new coat and a pampered place in the house. He dreamed his brothers and parents would look up to him. But what goes up must come down, and Joseph's life came down with a crash. Put down by his siblings. Thrown down into an empty well. Let down by his brothers and sold down the river as a slave. Then led down the road to Egypt.

Down, down, down. Stripped of name, status, position. Everything he had, everything he thought he'd ever have—gone. Vanished. Poof. Just like that.

Just like you? Have you been down in the mouth, down to your last dollar, down to the custody hearing, down to the bottom of the pecking order, down on your luck, down on your life . . . down . . . down to Egypt?

Life pulls us down.

Joseph arrived in Egypt with nothing. Not a penny to his name or a name worth a penny. His family tree was meaningless. His occupation was despised.[3] The clean-shaven people of the pyramids avoided the woolly Bedouins of the desert.

No credentials to stand on. No vocation to call on. No family to lean on. He had lost everything, with one exception: his destiny. A slight source of hope, but something.

Those odd dreams had convinced Joseph that God had plans for him. The details were vague and ill defined, for sure. Joseph had no way of knowing the specifics of his future. But the dreams told him this much: He would have a place of prominence in the midst of his family. Joseph latched on to this dream for the life jacket it was.

How else do we explain his survival? The Bible says nothing about his training, education, superior skills, or talents. But the narrator made a lead story out of Joseph's destiny.

The Hebrew boy lost his family, dignity, and home country, but he never lost his belief in God's belief in him. Trudging through the desert toward Egypt, he resolved, *It won't end this way. God has a dream for my life.* While wearing the heavy chains of the slave owners, he remembered, *I've been called to more than this.* Dragged into a city of strange tongues and shaved faces, he told himself, *God has greater plans for me.*

God had a destiny for Joseph, and the boy believed in it.

Do you believe in God's destiny for you?

I'm nearing half a century as a pastor. Fifty years is

plenty of time to hear Joseph stories. I've met many Egypt-bound people. Down, down, down. I've learned the question to ask. If you and I were having this talk over coffee, this is the point where I would lean across the table and say, "What do you still have that you cannot lose?" The difficulties have taken much away. I get that. But there is one gift your troubles cannot touch: your destiny. Can we talk about it?

You are God's child. He saw you, picked you, and placed you. The choice wasn't obligatory, required, compulsory, forced, or compelled. He selected you because he wanted to. You are his open, willful, voluntary choice. He walked onto the auction block where you stood, and he proclaimed, "This child is mine." And he bought you "with the precious blood of Christ, as of a lamb without blemish and without spot" (1 Peter 1:19). You are God's child.

You are his child *forever*.

Don't believe the tombstone. You are more than a dash between two dates. "When this tent we live in— our body here on earth—is torn down, God will have a house in heaven for us to live in, a home he himself has made, which will last forever" (2 Cor. 5:1 GNT). Don't get sucked into short-term thinking. Your struggles will not last forever, but you will.

God will have his Eden. He is creating a garden in which Adams and Eves will share in his likeness and love, at peace with each other, animals, and nature. We will rule with him over lands, cities, and nations. "If we endure, we shall also reign with Him" (2 Tim. 2:12).

> Don't get sucked into short-term thinking. Your struggles will not last forever, but you will.

Believe this. Clutch it. Tattoo it on the interior of your heart. It may seem that the calamity sucked your life out to sea, but it hasn't. You still have your destiny.

My father walked the road to Egypt. Family didn't betray him; his health did. He had just retired. He and Mom had saved their money and made their plans. They wanted to drive their travel trailer to visit every national park. Then came the diagnosis: amyotrophic lateral sclerosis (ALS, or Lou Gehrig's disease), a cruel degenerative disease that affects the muscles. Within months he was unable to feed, dress, or bathe himself. His world, as he knew it, was gone.

At the time, my wife, Denalyn, and I were preparing to do mission work in Brazil. When we got the news, I offered to change my plans. How could I leave the country while he was dying? Dad's reply was immediate and confident. He was not known for his long letters, but this one took up four pages and included the following imperative:

> In regard to my disease and your going to Rio. That is really an easy answer for me, and that is *Go*. . . . I have no fear of death or eternity . . . so don't be concerned about me. Just *Go*. Please him.

Dad lost much: his health, retirement, years with his children and grandchildren, years with his wife. The loss was severe, but it wasn't complete. "Dad," I could have asked, "what do you have that you cannot lose?" He still had God's call on his heart.

We forget this on the road to Egypt. Forgotten destinies litter the landscape like carcasses. We redefine ourselves according to our catastrophes. "I am the divorcée, the addict, the bankrupt businessperson, the kid with the disability, or the man with the scar." We settle for a small destiny: to make money, make friends, make a name, make muscle, or make love with anyone and everyone.

Determine not to make this mistake. Think you have lost it all? You haven't. "God's gifts and God's call are under full warranty—never canceled, never rescinded" (Rom. 11:29 MSG). Hear and heed yours.

Here's how it works. Your company is laying off employees. Your boss finally calls you into his office. As kind as he tries to be, a layoff is a layoff. All of a sudden you are cleaning out your desk. Internal voices of doubt and fear raise their volume. *How will I pay the bills? Who is going to hire me?* Dread dominates your thoughts. But then you remember your destiny: *What do I have that I cannot lose?*

Wait a second. I am still God's child. My life is more than this life. These days are a vapor, a passing breeze. This will eventually pass. God will make something good out of this. I will work hard, stay faithful, and trust him no matter what.

Bingo. You just trusted your destiny.

Try this one. Your fiancé wants his engagement ring back. All those promises and the proposal melted the moment he met the new girl at work. The jerk. The bum. The no-good pond scum. Like Joseph, you've been dumped into the pit. And, like Joseph, you choose to heed the call of God on your life. It's not easy. You're tempted to get even. But you choose instead to ponder your destiny. *I am God's child. My life is more than this life . . . more than this broken heart. This is God's promise, and unlike that sorry excuse for a guy, God won't break a promise.*

Another victory for God.

Another opportunity for hope.

Another reason to never give up.

Survival in Egypt begins with a yes to God's call on your life.

Several years after Dad's death I received a letter from a woman who remembered him. Ginger was only six years old when her Sunday school class made get-well cards for ailing church members. She created a bright purple card out of construction paper and carefully lined it with stickers. On the inside she wrote, "I love you, but most of all God loves you." Her mom baked a pie, and the two made the delivery.

Dad was bedfast. The end was near. His jaw tended to drop, leaving his mouth open. He could extend his hand, but it was bent to a claw from the disease.

Somehow Ginger had a moment alone with him and asked a question as only a six-year-old can: "Are you going to die?"

He touched her hand and told her to come near. "Yes, I am going to die. When? I don't know."

She asked if he was afraid to go away. "Away is heaven," he told her. "I will be with my Father. I am ready to see him eye to eye."

About this point in the visit, her mother and mine returned. Ginger recalls,

My mother consoled your parents with a fake smile on her face. But I smiled a big, beautiful, *real* smile, and he did the same and winked at me.

My purpose for telling you all this is my family and I are going to Kenya. We are going to take Jesus to a tribe on the coast. I am very scared for my children, because I know there will be hardships and disease. But for me, I am not afraid, because the worst thing that could happen is getting to see "my Father eye to eye."

It was your father who taught me that earth is only a passing through and death is merely a rebirth.

A man near death winking at the thought of it. Stripped of everything? It only appeared that way. In the end Dad still had what no one could take. And in the end that is all he needed.

—— REFLECTION QUESTIONS ——

1. How would you explain what you believe to be God's destiny for your life?

2. In Egypt, Joseph had lost everything except his destiny—his God-given identity and purpose. How would you summarize that destiny?

3. One way to think about destiny is that we already know the ending of the story—God's and our own—and it is deeply good. What can you say for certain about the ending of your own story? Your eternal destiny?

4. Think back over the past week. What were some specific moments you experienced God's goodness and grace extended toward you? Write down as many as come to mind.

5. How would you describe your own God-given identity and purpose? What has God called you to hang on to when everything else may seem to be slipping away?

6. Where do you have an opportunity right now to say yes to hope? To refuse to give up?

THREE

DOWN TO THE BOTTOM

Melanie Jasper says her son, Cooper, was born with a smile on his face. The dimple never left his cheek. He won the hearts of every person he knew: his three older sisters, parents, grandparents, teachers, and friends. He loved to laugh and love. His father, JJ, confessing partiality, calls him practically a perfect child.

And Cooper was born to the perfect family. Farm-dwelling, fun-loving, God-seeking, and Christ-hungry, JJ and Melanie poured their hearts into their four children. JJ cherished every moment he had with his only son. That's why they were in the dune buggy on that summer day. They intended to cut the grass together, but the lawn mower needed a spark plug. While Melanie drove to town to buy one, JJ and five-year-old Cooper seized the opportunity for a quick ride. They had done this a thousand times, zipping down a dirt road in a roll cage cart. The ride was nothing new. But the flip was. On a completely level road with Cooper safely buckled in, JJ made a circle, and the buggy rolled over.

Cooper was unresponsive. JJ called 911, then Melanie. "There's been an accident," he told her. "I don't think Cooper is going to make it." The next hours were every parent's worst nightmare: ambulance, ER, sobs, and shock. And finally, the news. Cooper had passed from this life into heaven. JJ and Melanie found themselves doing the unthinkable: selecting a casket, planning a funeral, and envisioning life without their only son. In the coming days they fell into a mind-numbing rhythm. Each morning upon awakening they held each other and sobbed uncontrollably. After gathering enough courage to climb out of bed, they would go downstairs to the family and friends who awaited them. They would soldier through the day until bedtime. Then they would go to bed, hold each other, and cry themselves to sleep.

JJ told me, "There is no class or book on this planet that can prepare you to have your five-year-old son die in your arms . . . We know what the bottom looks like."[4]

The bottom. We pass much of life—if not most of life—at mid-altitude. Occasionally we summit a peak: our wedding, a promotion, the birth of a child. But most of life is lived at midlevel. Mondayish obligations of carpools, expense reports, and recipes.

But on occasion the world bottoms out. The dune buggy flips, the housing market crashes, the test results come back positive, and before we know it, we discover what the bottom looks like.

In Joseph's case he discovered the auction block of Egypt. The bidding began, and for the second time in his young life, he was on the market. The favored son of Jacob found himself prodded and pricked, examined for fleas, and pushed about like a donkey. Potiphar, an Egyptian officer, bought him. Joseph didn't speak the language or know the culture. The food was strange, the work was grueling, and the odds were against him.

So we turn the page and brace for the worst. The next chapter in his story will describe Joseph's consequential plunge into addiction, anger, or despair, right? Wrong.

"The LORD was with Joseph, and he was a successful man; and he was in the house of his master the Egyptian" (Gen. 39:2). Joseph arrived in Egypt with nothing but the clothes on his back and the call of God on his heart. Yet by the end of four verses, he was running the house of the man who ran security for Pharaoh. How do we explain this turnaround? Simple. God was with him.

The LORD was with Joseph, and he was a successful man. (Gen. 39:2)

His master saw that the LORD was with him. (v. 3)

The LORD blessed the Egyptian's house for Joseph's sake. (v. 5)

The blessing of the LORD was on all that he had. (v. 5)

Joseph's story just parted company with the volumes of self-help books and all the secret-to-success formulas that direct the struggler to an inner power ("dig deeper"). Joseph's story points elsewhere ("look higher"). He succeeded because God was present. God was to Joseph what a blanket is to a baby—he was all over him.

Any chance he'd be the same for you? Here you are in your version of Egypt. It feels foreign. You don't know the language. You never studied the vocabulary of crisis. You feel far from home, all alone. Money gone. Expectations dashed. Friends vanished. Who's left? God is.

David asked, "Where can I go to get away from your Spirit? Where can I run from you?" (Ps. 139:7 NCV). He then listed the various places he found God: in "the heavens . . . the grave. . . . If I rise with the sun in the east and settle in the west beyond the sea, even there you would guide me" (Ps. 139:8–10 NCV). God, everywhere.

Joseph's account of those verses would have read, "Where can I go to get away from your Spirit? If I go to the bottom of the dry pit . . . to the top of the slave block . . . to the home of a foreigner . . . even there you would guide me."

Your adaptation of the verse might read, "Where can I go to get away from your Spirit? If I go to the rehab clinic . . . the ICU . . . the overseas deployment office . . . the shelter for battered women . . . the county jail . . . even there you would guide me."

You will never go where God is not. Make God's presence your passion.

How? Be more sponge and less rock. Place a rock in the ocean, and what happens? Its surface gets wet. The exterior may change color, but the interior remains untouched. Yet place a sponge in the ocean and notice the change. It absorbs the water. The ocean penetrates every pore and alters the essence of the sponge.

God surrounds us in the same way the Pacific surrounds an ocean floor pebble. He is everywhere—above, below, on all sides. We choose our response: Rock or

You will never go where God is not. Make God's presence your passion.

sponge? Resist or receive? Everything within you says harden the heart. *Run from God; resist God; blame God.* But be careful. Hard hearts never heal. Spongy ones do.

Here's how to open every pore of your soul to God's presence: *Lay claim to the nearness of God.* "Never will I leave you; never will I forsake you" (Heb. 13:5 NIV). In the Greek this passage has five negatives. It could be translated "I will not, not leave thee; neither will I not, not forsake thee."[5] Grip this promise like the parachute it is. Repeat it to yourself over and over until it trumps the voices of fear and angst. "The LORD your God is with you, the Mighty Warrior who saves. He will take great delight in you; in his love he will no longer rebuke you, but will rejoice over you with singing" (Zeph. 3:17 NIV).

You may lose the *sense* of God's presence. Job did. "But if I go to the east, he is not there; if I go to the west, I do not find him. When he is at work in the north, I do not see him; when he turns to the south, I catch no glimpse of him" (Job 23:8–9 NIV). Job *felt* far from God. Yet in spite of his inability to feel God, Job resolved, "But he knows the way that I take; when he has tested me, I will come forth as gold" (v. 10 NIV). What gritty determination. Difficult days demand decisions of faith.

The psalmist determined,

Down to the Bottom

When I am afraid,
I put my trust in you. (Ps. 56:3 NIV)

Why, my soul, are you downcast?
Why so disturbed within me?
Put your hope in God,
for *I will yet praise* him. (Ps. 42:5 NIV)

Don't equate the presence of God with a good mood or a pleasant temperament. God is near whether you are happy or not. Sometimes you have to take your feelings outside and give them a good talking-to.

Cling to his character. Quarry from your Bible a list of the deep qualities of God and press them into your heart. My list reads like this:

He is still sovereign.
He still knows my name.
Angels still respond to his call.
The hearts of rulers still yield to his bidding.
The death of Jesus still saves souls.
The Spirit of God still indwells saints.
Heaven is still only heartbeats away.
The grave is still temporary housing.
God is still faithful.

He is not caught off guard.
He uses everything for his glory and my
     ultimate good.
He uses tragedy to accomplish his will, and his will
     is right, holy, and perfect.
Sorrow may come with the night, but joy comes
     with the morning.
God bears fruit in the midst of a-ffliction.

When JJ Jasper told his oldest daughter about Cooper's death, he prepared her by saying, "I need you to hold on to everything you know of who God is, because I have some really tough news to tell you." What valuable counsel!

In changing times, lay hold of the unchanging character of God.

> When all around my soul gives way,
> He then is all my hope and stay.[6]

In changing times, lay hold of the unchanging character of God.

Pray your pain out. Pound the table. March up and down the lawn. It's time for tenacious, honest prayers. Angry at God? Disappointed with his strategy? Ticked off at his choices? Let him know it. Let him have it! Jeremiah did. This ancient prophet pastored Jerusalem during a time of economic collapse and political upheaval. Invasion. Disaster. Exile. Hunger. Death. Jeremiah saw it all. He so filled his devotions with complaints that his prayer journal is called Lamentations.

> [God] has led me and made me walk
> In darkness and not in light.
> Surely He has turned His hand against me
> Time and time again throughout the day.
> He has aged my flesh and my skin,
> And broken my bones.
> He has besieged me
> And surrounded me with bitterness and woe.
> He has set me in dark places
> Like the dead of long ago.
> He has hedged me in so that I cannot get out;
> He has made my chain heavy.
> Even when I cry and shout,
> He shuts out my prayer. (Lam. 3:2–8)

Jeremiah infused five chapters with this type of fury. You could summarize the bulk of his book with one line: This life is rotten! Why would God place Lamentations in the Bible? Might it be to convince you to follow Jeremiah's example?

Go ahead and file your grievance. "I pour out my complaint before him; I tell my trouble before him" (Ps. 142:2 ESV). God will not turn away at your anger. Even Jesus offered up prayers with "fervent cries and tears" (Heb. 5:7 NIV). It is better to shake a fist at God than to turn your back on him. Augustine said, "How deep in the deep are they who do not cry out of the deep."[7]

Words might seem hollow and empty at first. You will mumble your sentences, fumble your thoughts. But don't quit. And don't hide.

Lean on God's people. Cancel your escape to the Himalayas. Forget the deserted island. This is no time to be a hermit. Be a barnacle on the boat of God's church. "For where two or three are gathered together in My name, *I am there* in the midst of them" (Matt. 18:20).

Would the sick avoid the hospital? The hungry avoid the food pantry? The discouraged abandon God's Hope Distribution Center? Only at great risk. His people purvey his presence.

JJ Jasper found God's presence amid God's people. His hurts are still deep, but his faith is deeper still. Whenever he tells the story of losing Cooper, he says this: "We know what the bottom looks like, and we know who is waiting there—Jesus Christ."

He's waiting on you, my friend. If Joseph's story is

any precedent, God can use Egypt to teach you that he is with you. Your family may be gone. Your supporters may have left. Your counselor may be silent. But God has not budged. His promise still stands: "I am with you and will watch over you wherever you go" (Gen. 28:15 NIV).

—— REFLECTION QUESTIONS ——

1. When you experience or read about an unimaginable tragedy, what sustains you and brings you hope?

2. Genesis 39:1–6 emphasizes several times that God was "with" Joseph. What does that mean? How have you experienced that phenomenon in your life?

3. One way we can open ourselves to God's presence is to *lay claim to the nearness of God*. What would it look like for you to assume God is near you each day? To claim that reality?

4. We can also *cling to God's character*. What are some things you know to be true about God— who he is, what he values, what he does, and so

on? Write down as many answers as you can in the next two minutes.

5. A third way of remaining open to God is to *pray your pain out*, as Jeremiah did in his Lamentations. How often do you speak honestly with God about what you are feeling? How often do you speak openly about your anger, doubts, fears, or pain?

6. A final method for opening ourselves to God is to *lean on God's people*. Where do you have an opportunity right now to reach out to people in your faith community who can offer you support? Where do you have an opportunity to support someone in need?

FOUR

THIS IS A TEST

On November 28, 1965, Howard Rutledge's fighter plane exploded under enemy fire. He parachuted into the hands of the North Vietnamese Army and was promptly placed in the "Heartbreak Hotel," one of the prisons in Hanoi.

When the door slammed and the key turned in that rusty, iron lock, a feeling of utter loneliness swept over me. I lay down on that cold cement slab in my 6 x 6 prison. The smell of human excrement burned my nostrils. A rat, large as a small cat, scampered across the slab beside me. The walls and floors and ceilings were caked with filth. Bars covered a tiny window high above the door. I was cold and hungry; my body ached from the swollen joints and sprained muscles. . . .

It's hard to describe what solitary confinement can do to unnerve and defeat a man. You quickly tire of standing up or sitting down, sleeping or being awake. There are no books, no paper or pencils, no magazines or newspapers. The only colors you see are drab gray and dirty brown. Months or years may go by when you don't see the sunrise or the moon, green grass or flowers. You are locked in, alone and silent in your filthy little cell breathing stale, rotten air and trying to keep your sanity.[8]

Few of us will ever face the austere conditions of a POW camp. Yet to one degree or another, we all spend time behind bars.

- My email contains a prayer request for a young mother just diagnosed with lupus. Incarcerated by bad health.
- I had coffee with a man whose wife battles depression. He feels stuck (chain number one) and guilty for feeling stuck (chain number two).
- After half a century of marriage, a friend's wife began to lose her memory and her health. He had to take away her car keys. He has to stay near so she won't fall. They had hopes of growing old

together. They still may, but only one of them will know the day of the week and remember their life before dementia.

Each of these individuals wonders, *Where is heaven in this story? Why would God permit such imprisonment? Does this struggle serve any purpose?* Joseph surely posed those questions to himself as he slumped behind his prison bars.

Joseph spent time in jail. Here's the backstory.

In the household of Potiphar, Joseph moved up the career ladder like a fireman after a cat. He earned promotions. He earned clout. He earned attention—too much attention, in fact. It didn't take long for Mrs. Potiphar to notice this handsome young Hebrew and to make her intentions crystal clear. "And it came to pass after these things that his master's wife cast longing eyes on Joseph, and she said, 'Lie with me'" (Gen. 39:7). Verse 10 says she courted him "day by day."

Joseph had plenty of opportunities to consider the proposition. And reasons to accept it. After all, wasn't she married to his master? And wasn't he obligated to obey the wishes of his owner, even if the wish was clandestine sex? And it *would be* clandestine. No one would know. What happens in the bedroom stays in the bedroom, right? And didn't Joseph deserve a little pleasure after everything he'd experienced? A little comfort? A little release?

But no. Adultery would have been only another form of abandoning his destiny. Another way of giving up. So young Joseph held firm.

Unfortunately, so did Mrs. Potiphar. If she couldn't flirt Joseph into her bed, she would force him. She grabbed for his robe, and he let her have it. He chose his character over his coat. When he ran, she concocted a story. When Potiphar came home, she was ready with her lie and Joseph's coat as proof. Potiphar charged Joseph with sexual assault and locked him in jail. "And [Joseph] was there in the prison. But the LORD was with Joseph and showed him mercy, and He gave him favor in the sight of the keeper of the prison" (Gen. 39:20–21).

Not a prison in the modern sense but a warren of underground, windowless rooms with damp floors, stale food, and bitter water. Guards shoved him into the dungeon and slammed the door. Joseph leaned back against the wall, slid to the floor. "I have done nothing here that they should put me into the dungeon" (40:15).

Joseph had done his best in Potiphar's house. He had made a fortune for his employer. He had kept his chores done and his room tidy. He had adapted to a new culture. He had resisted the sexual advances. But how was he rewarded? A prison sentence with no hope of parole. Since when does the high road lead over a cliff?

The answer? Ever since the events of Genesis 3, the chapter that documents the entry of evil into the world. Disaster came in the form of Lucifer, the fallen angel. And as long as Satan "prowls around like a roaring lion" (1 Peter 5:8 NIV), he will wreak havoc among God's people. He will lock preachers, like Paul, in prisons. He will exile pastors, like John, on remote islands. He will afflict the friends of Jesus, like Lazarus, with diseases. But his strategies always backfire. The imprisoned Paul wrote epistles. The banished John saw heaven. The cemetery of Lazarus became a stage on which Christ performed one of his greatest miracles.

Intended evil becomes ultimate good.

Remember, God is not *sometimes* sovereign. He is not *occasionally* victorious. He does not occupy the throne one day and vacate it the next. "The LORD will not turn back until He has fulfilled and until He has accomplished the intent of His heart (mind)" (Jer. 30:24 AMP). This season in which you find yourself may puzzle you, but it does not bewilder God. He can and will use it for his purpose.

Case in point: Joseph in prison. From an earthly

This season in which you find yourself may puzzle you, but it does not bewilder God. He can and will use it for his purpose.

viewpoint the Egyptian jail was the tragic conclusion of Joseph's life. Satan could chalk up a victory for the dark side. All plans to use Joseph ended with the slamming of the jail door. The devil had Joseph just where he wanted him. So did God.

> They bruised [Joseph's] feet with fetters
> and placed his neck in an iron collar.
> Until the time came to fulfill his dreams,
> the LORD *tested* Joseph's character.
> (Ps. 105:18–19 NLT)

What Satan intended for evil, God used for testing. In the Bible, a test is an external trial that purifies and prepares the heart. Just as a fire refines precious metal from dross and impurities, a trial purges the heart of the same. One of the psalmists wrote,

> For you, O God, tested us;
> you refined us like silver.
> You brought us into prison
> and laid burdens on our backs.
> You let people ride over our heads;

> we went through fire and water,
> but you brought us to a place of abundance.
> (Ps. 66:10–12 NIV)

Every day God tests us through people, pain, or problems. Stop and consider your circumstances. Can you identify the tests of today? Snarling traffic? Threatening weather? Aching joints?

If you see your troubles as nothing more than isolated hassles and hurts, you'll grow bitter and angry. Yet if you see your troubles as tests used by God for his glory and your maturity, then even the smallest incidents take on significance.

I remember one Saturday afternoon that turned into a tough test. Denalyn and I had a disagreement. We had agreed to sell our house, but we couldn't agree on a real estate agent. I had my opinion, and she had hers. Back and forth we went, neither able to convince the other. A pleasant day turned sour. She retreated into her corner and I into mine.

We have Saturday worship services at our church. When the time came for me to leave and preach, I gave Denalyn a perfunctory goodbye and walked out the door to do God's work. "We'll deal with this later," I told her.

But God wanted to deal with me immediately. The

distance between my house and the church building is only a five-minute drive. But that is all it took for God to prick my conscience with the truth. *Shouldn't you be at peace with your wife before you preach to my church?*

It was a test. Would I pout or apologize? Would I ignore the tension or deal with it? I can't say I always pass the tests, but that day I did with flying colors. Before the service began, I called Denalyn, apologized for my stubbornness, and asked for her forgiveness. Later that night we reached a decision on a real estate agent. We prayed together and put the matter to rest.

Each day has a pop quiz. And some seasons are final exams. Brutal, sudden pitfalls of stress, sickness, or sadness. Like Joseph, you did your best. Like Joseph, your best was rewarded with incarceration. What is the purpose of the test? Why didn't God keep Joseph out of prison? Might this be the answer? "For you know that when your faith is tested, your endurance has a chance to grow. So let it grow, for when your endurance is fully developed, you will be perfect and complete, needing nothing" (James 1:3–4 NLT).

As a boy Joseph was prone to softness. Jacob indulged him, spoiled him. Joseph talked about his dreams and grand ambitions. A bit too full of himself, perhaps. Even in Potiphar's house Joseph was the darling of the estate.

Quickly promoted, often noticed. Success came easily. Perhaps pride did as well. If so, a prison term would purge that. God knew the challenges that lay ahead, and he used Joseph's time in prison to strengthen his servant.

"And the keeper of the prison committed to Joseph's hand all the prisoners who were in the prison; whatever they did there, it was his doing" (Gen. 39:22). Talk about a crash course in leadership! Joseph managed willing servants for Potiphar. But in prison he was assigned unruly, disrespectful, and ungrateful men. Joseph could have cloistered himself in a corner and mumbled, "I've learned my lesson. I'm not running anything for anybody." But he didn't complain, didn't criticize.

In short, he didn't give up. He displayed a willing spirit with the prisoners—and with God.

He was especially kind to a butler and a baker. The butler and the baker, both officers of Pharaoh, were placed in Joseph's care. One morning he noticed deep frowns on their faces. He could have dismissed their expressions. What concern was their sorrow to him? Who cared if they were sullen or bitter? Joseph, however, took an interest in them. In fact, the first recorded words of Joseph in the prison were kind ones: "Why do you look so sad?" (Gen. 40:7). Abandoned by his brothers, sold into slavery, and unjustly imprisoned, Joseph was still tender toward others. Wouldn't compassion be a suitable quality for the soon-to-be director of a worldwide hunger-relief program?

God wasn't finished. Both the baker and the butler were troubled by dreams. In his dream the butler saw a vine with three grape-bearing branches. He pressed the grapes into Pharaoh's cup and gave it to the king. The baker dreamed about bread. Three baskets were on his head, and birds ate the bread in the top basket. Both men sought Joseph's counsel. And Joseph received an interpretation from God. Would he share it? The last time Joseph spoke of dreams, he ended up in a dry cistern. Besides, only 50 percent of his revelation was good news. Could Joseph be trusted to share God's news? If called to stand before Pharaoh, would Joseph accurately convey God's word?

This was a test. Joseph passed it. He gave the butler good news ("You'll be out in three days") and the baker bad news ("You'll be dead in three days"). One would get a new start; the other, a noose around the neck.

Test, test, test. The dungeon looked like a prison, smelled like a prison, sounded like a prison. But had you asked the angels of heaven about Joseph's location, they would have replied, "Oh, he is in boot camp."

This chapter in your life looks like rehab, smells

like unemployment, sounds like a hospital, but ask the angels. "Oh, she is in training."

God hasn't forgotten you. Just the opposite. He has chosen to train you. The Hebrew verb for *test* comes from a word that means "to take a keen look at, to look, to choose."[9] Dismiss the notion that God does not see your struggle. On the contrary, God is fully engaged. He sees the needs of tomorrow and, accordingly, uses your circumstances to create the test of today.

> God hasn't forgotten you. Just the opposite. He has chosen to train you.

Does he not have the authority to do so? He is the Potter; we are the clay. He is the Shepherd; we are the sheep. He is the Gardener; we are the branches. He is the Teacher; we are the students. Trust his training. Don't give up. You'll get through this. If God can make a prince out of a prisoner, don't you think he can make something good out of your mess?

Remember, all tests are temporary. They are limited in duration. "In this you greatly rejoice, though now *for a little while* you may have had to suffer grief in all kinds of trials" (1 Peter 1:6 NIV). Tests never last forever, because this life doesn't last forever. "We were born but yesterday. . . . Our days on earth are as fleeting as a shadow"

(Job 8:9 NLT). Some tests end on earth, but all tests will end in heaven.

> Some tests end on earth, but all tests will end in heaven.

In the meantime, follow Joseph's example. Let God train you. He is watching the way you handle the little jobs. If you are faithful with a few matters, he will set you over many (Matt. 25:21). Joseph succeeded in the kitchen and dungeon before he succeeded in the court. He cared for the butler and baker before he cared for the nations. The reward of good work is greater work. Do you aspire to great things? Excel in the small things. Show up on time. Finish your work early. Don't complain. Let others grumble in the corner of the prison cell. Not you. You know how God shapes his servants. Today's prisoner may become tomorrow's prime minister. When you are given a task, take it on.

Life is a required course. Might as well do your best to pass it.

God is at work in each of us whether we know it or not, whether we want it or not. "He takes no pleasure in making life hard, in throwing roadblocks in the way" (Lam. 3:33 MSG). He does not relish our sufferings, but he delights in our development. "God began doing a good work in you, and I am sure he will continue it until it is finished when Jesus Christ comes again" (Phil. 1:6 NCV).

He will not fail. He cannot fail. He will "work in us what is pleasing to him" (Heb. 13:21 NIV). Every challenge, large or small, can equip you for a future opportunity.

Howard Rutledge came to appreciate his time as a POW in Vietnam. He wrote:

> During those long periods of enforced reflection, it became so much easier to separate the important from the trivial, the worthwhile from the waste. . . .
>
> My hunger for spiritual food soon outdid my hunger for a steak . . . I wanted to know about the part of me that will never die . . . I wanted to talk about God and Christ and the church . . . It took prison to show me how empty life is without God. . . .
>
> On August 31, after twenty-eight days of torture, I could remember I had children but not how many. I said Phyllis's name over and over again so I would not forget. I prayed for strength. It was on that twenty-eighth night I made God a promise. If I survived this ordeal, the first Sunday back in freedom I would take Phyllis and my family to their church and . . . confess my faith in Christ and join the church. This wasn't a deal with God to get me through that last miserable night. It was a promise made after months of thought. It took prison and

hours of painful reflection to realize how much I needed God and the community of believers. After I made God that promise, again I prayed for strength to make it through the night.

When the morning dawned through the crack in the bottom of that solid prison door, I thanked God for His mercy.[10]

Don't see your struggle as an interruption to life but as preparation for life. No one said the road would be easy or painless. But God will use this mess for something good. "This trouble you're in isn't punishment; it's *training*, the normal experience of children. . . . God is doing what *is* best for us, training us to live God's holy best" (Heb. 12:8, 10 MSG).

—— REFLECTION QUESTIONS ——

1. What are some tests you've faced in your lifetime? What were the results?

2. What do you consider the greatest test of your life? How did you handle the pressure of being tested?

3. Read Genesis 39:7–18. What were the stakes of Joseph's test during this season of his life? What did he have to gain or lose through his choices with Potiphar's wife?

4. Read Genesis 40:1–23. What were the stakes of Joseph's test during this season of his life? What did he have to gain or lose through his interactions with the butler and the baker?

5. Do you ever lay your tests before God? What would doing this mean for you?

6. We all have the ability to share our testimony—our story. What can you say about the way God has loved you and cared for you in the midst of a mess?

FIVE

GOD'S WAITING ROOM

Here I sit in the waiting room. The receptionist took my name, recorded my insurance data, and gestured to a chair. "Please have a seat. We will call you when the doctor is ready." I look around. A mother holds a sleeping baby. A fellow dressed in a suit thumbs through *Time* magazine. A woman with a newspaper looks at her watch, sighs, and continues the task of the hour: waiting.

The waiting room. Not the examination room. That's down the hall. Not the consultation room. That's on the other side of the wall. Not the treatment room. Exams, consultations, and treatments all come later.

The task at hand is the name of the room: the waiting room. We in the waiting room understand our assignment: to wait. We don't treat each other. I don't ask the nurse for a stethoscope or blood pressure cuff. I don't pull up a chair next to the woman with the newspaper and say, "Tell me what prescriptions you are taking." That's the job of the nurse. My job is to wait. So I do.

Can't say that I like it. Time moves like an Alaskan glacier. The clock ticks every five minutes, not every second. Someone pressed the pause button. Life in slo-mo. We don't like to wait. We are the giddy-up generation. We weave through traffic, looking for the faster lane. We frown at the person who takes eleven items into the ten-item express checkout. We drum our fingers while the video downloads or the microwave heats our coffee. "Come on, come on." We want six-pack abs in ten minutes and minute rice in thirty seconds. We don't like to wait. Not on the doctor, the traffic, or the pizza.

Not on God?

Take a moment and look around you. Do you realize where we sit? This planet is God's waiting room.

The young couple in the corner? Waiting to get pregnant. The fellow with the briefcase? He has résumés all over the country, waiting on work. The elderly woman with the cane? A widow. Been waiting a year for one tearless day. Waiting. Waiting on God to give, help, heal. Waiting on God to come. We indwell the land betwixt prayer offered and prayer answered. The land of waiting.

If anyone knew the furniture of God's waiting

room, Joseph did. One problem with reading his story is its brevity. We can read the Genesis account from start to finish in less than an hour, which gives the impression that all these challenges took place before breakfast one morning. We'd be wiser to pace our reading over a couple of decades.

Take chapter 37 into a dry cistern and sit there for a couple of hours while the sun beats down. Recite the first verse of chapter 39 over and over for a couple of months: "Now Joseph had been taken down to Egypt." Joseph needed at least this much time to walk the 750 miles from Dothan to Thebes.

Then there was the day or days or weeks on the auction block. Add to that probably a decade in Potiphar's house, supervising the servants, doing his master's bidding, learning Egyptian. Tick tock. Tick tock. Tick tock. Time moves slowly in a foreign land.

And time stands still in a prison.

Joseph had asked the butler to put in a good word for him. "Remember me when it is well with you, and please show kindness to me; make mention of me to Pharaoh, and get me out of this house. . . . I have done nothing here that they should put me into the dungeon" (Gen. 40:14–15).

We can almost hear the butler reply, "Certainly, I

will mention you to Pharaoh. First chance I get. You'll be hearing from me." Joseph hurried back to his cell and collected his belongings. He wanted to be ready when the call came. A day passed. Then two. Then a week. A month. Six months. No word. As it turned out, Pharaoh's butler "did not remember Joseph, but forgot him" (Gen. 40:23).

On the page of your Bible, the un-inked space between that verse and the next is scarcely wider than a hair ribbon. It takes your eyes only a split second to see it. Yet it took Joseph two years to experience it. Chapter 41 starts like this: "Two years passed and Pharaoh had a dream" (v. 1 MSG).

Two years! Twenty-four months of silence. One hundred and four weeks of waiting. Seven hundred and thirty days of wondering. Two thousand one hundred and ninety meals alone. Seventeen thousand five hundred and twenty hours of listening for God yet hearing nothing but silence.

Plenty of time to grow bitter, cynical, angry. Folks have given up on God for lesser reasons in shorter times.

Not Joseph. On a day that began like any other, he heard a stirring at the dungeon entrance. Loud, impatient voices demanded, "We are here for the Hebrew! Pharaoh wants the Hebrew!" Joseph looked up from his corner to see the prison master, white-faced and stammering. "Get up! Hurry, get up!" Two guards from the court were on his heels. Joseph remembered them from his days in Potiphar's service. They took him by the elbows and marched him out of the hole. He squinted at the brilliant sunlight. They walked him across a courtyard into a room. Attendants flocked around him. They removed his soiled clothing, washed his body, and shaved his beard. They dressed him in a white robe and new sandals. The guards reappeared and walked him into the throne room.

And so it was that Joseph and Pharaoh looked into each other's eyes for the first time.

Dreams had kept Pharaoh up half the night. In dream number one, cows grazed on the riverbank. Seven were fine and fat, prime candidates for a Chick-fil-A commercial. But while the healthy bovines weren't looking, seven skinny cows sneaked up from behind and devoured them. Pharaoh woke up in a sweat.

Dream number two was just as bothersome. A stalk of grain with seven healthy heads was consumed by a stalk of grain with seven withered heads. Two dreams with the same pattern: The seven bad devoured the seven good.

Pharaoh was upset. The prisoner was unfazed.

Joseph heard the dreams and went straight to work. No need to consult advisers or tea leaves. This was simple stuff, like basic multiplication for a Harvard math professor. "Expect seven years of plenty and seven years of famine."

Famine was a foul word in the Egyptian dictionary. The nation didn't manufacture Chevys or export T-shirts. Their civilization was built on farms. Crops made Egypt the jewel of the Nile. Agriculture made Pharaoh the most powerful man in the world. A monthlong drought would hurt the economy. A year-long famine would weaken the throne of Pharaoh, who owned the fields around the Nile. A seven-year famine would turn the Nile into a creek and the crops to sticks. Apocalypse!

The silence in the throne room was so thick you could hear a cough drop. Joseph took advantage of the pause in conversation to offer a solution. "Create a department of agriculture, and commission a smart person to gather grain in the good years and to distribute it during the lean years."

Officials gulped at Joseph's chutzpah. It was one thing to give bad news to Pharaoh, another to offer unsolicited advice. Yet the guy hadn't shown a hint of fear since he entered the palace. He paid no homage to the king. He didn't offer accolades to the magicians. He didn't kiss rings or polish apples. Lesser men would have cowered. Joseph didn't blink.

Again the contrast. The most powerful person in the room, Pharaoh (ruler of the Nile, deity of the heavens, Grand Pooh-Bah of the pyramid people), was sweating. The lowest person in the pecking order, Joseph (ex-slave, convict, accused sex offender), was cooler than the other side of the pillow.

What made the difference? Ballast. Joseph's life was built on a foundation; it was anchored on the deep-seated, stabilizing belief in God's sovereignty.

We sense it in his first sentence: "It is not in me; God will give Pharaoh an answer of peace" (Gen. 41:16). The second time Joseph spoke, he explained: "God has shown Pharaoh what He is about to do" (v. 28). Joseph proceeded to interpret the dreams and then tell Pharaoh that the dreams were "established by God, and God will shortly bring it to pass" (v. 32).

Four times in three verses Joseph made reference to God! "God . . . God . . . God . . . God."

In other words, Joseph emerged from his prison cell bragging on God. Jail time didn't devastate his faith; it deepened it.

And you? You aren't in prison, but you may be

*in*fertile or *in*active or *in* limbo or *in* between jobs or *in* search of health, help, a house, or a spouse. Are you in God's waiting room? If so, here is what you need to know: *While you wait, God works.*

"My Father is always at his work," Jesus said (John 5:17 NIV). God never twiddles his thumbs. He never stops. He takes no vacations. He rested on the seventh day of creation but got back to work on the eighth and hasn't stopped since. Just because you are idle, don't assume God is.

While you wait, God works.

Joseph's story appeared to stall out in chapter 40. Our hero was in shackles. The train was off the tracks. History was in a holding pattern. But while Joseph was waiting, God was working. He assembled the characters. God placed the butler in Joseph's care. He stirred the sleep of the king with odd dreams. He confused Pharaoh's counselors. And at just the right time, God called Joseph to duty.

He's working for you as well. "Be still, and know that I am God"[11] reads the sign on God's waiting room wall. You can be glad because God is good. You can be still because he is active. You can rest because he is busy.

To wait, biblically speaking, is not to assume the worst, worry, fret, make demands, or take control. Nor is waiting inactivity. Waiting is a sustained effort to stay focused on God through prayer and belief. To wait is to "rest in the LORD, and wait patiently for Him" and to "not fret" (Ps. 37:7).

Waiting is easier read than done. It doesn't come easily for me. I've been in a hurry my whole life. Hurrying to school, hurrying to finish homework. Pedal faster, drive quicker. I used to put my wristwatch face on the inside of my arm so I wouldn't lose the millisecond it took to turn my wrist. What insanity! I wonder if I could have obeyed God's ancient command to keep the Sabbath holy. To slow life to a crawl for twenty-four hours. The Sabbath was created for frantic souls like me, people who need this weekly reminder: The world will not stop if you do!

And what of this command: "Three times a year all your men are to appear before the Sovereign LORD, the God of Israel. I will drive out nations before you and enlarge your territory, and no one will covet your land when you go up three times each year to appear before the LORD your God" (Ex. 34:23–24 NIV)? God instructed the promised land settlers to stop their work three times a year and gather for worship. All commerce, education, government, and industry came to a halt while the people assembled. Can you imagine this happening today? Our country would be utterly defenseless.

Yet God promised to protect the territory. No one would encroach on the Israelites. What's more, they wouldn't even desire to do so. "No one will covet your land." God used the pilgrimage to teach this principle: If you will wait in worship, I will work for you.

Daniel did this. In one of the most dramatic examples of waiting in the Bible, this Old Testament prophet kept his mind on God for an extended period. His people had been oppressed for almost seventy years. Daniel entered into a time of prayer on their behalf. For twenty-one days he abstained from pleasant food, meat, and wine. He labored in prayer. He persisted, pleaded, and agonized.

No response.

Then, on the twenty-second day, a breakthrough. An angel of God appeared. He revealed to Daniel the reason for the long delay. Daniel's prayer was heard on the first day it was offered. The angel was dispatched with a response. "That very day I was sent here to meet you. But for twenty-one days the mighty Evil Spirit who overrules the kingdom of Persia blocked my way. Then Michael, one of the top officers of the heavenly army, came to help me, so that I was able to break through these spirit rulers of Persia" (Dan. 10:12–13 TLB).

From an earthly perspective nothing was happening.

Daniel's prayers were falling like pebbles on hard ground. But from a heavenly perspective a battle was raging in the heavens. Two angels were engaged in fierce combat for three weeks. While Daniel was waiting, God was working.

What if Daniel had given up? Lost faith? Walked away from God?

Better questions: What if you give up? Lose faith? Walk away?

Don't. For heaven's sake, never give up! All of heaven is warring on your behalf. Above and around you at this very instant, God's messengers are at work.

Keep waiting.

> Those who wait on the LORD
> Shall renew their strength;
> They shall mount up with wings like
>   eagles,
> They shall run and not be weary,
> They shall walk and not faint. (Isa. 40:31)

For heaven's sake, never give up! All of heaven is warring on your behalf.

Fresh strength. Renewed vigor. Legs that don't grow weary. Delight yourself in God, and he will bring rest to your soul.

You'll get through this waiting room season just fine.

Pay careful note, and you will detect the most wonderful surprise. The doctor will step out of his office and take the seat next to yours. "Just thought I'd keep you company while you are waiting." Not every physician will do that, but yours will. After all, he is the Great Physician.

—— REFLECTION QUESTIONS ——

1. In your life, what "waiting" situations have been most challenging? How do you manage your waiting moments or seasons?

2. Joseph spent thirteen years in Egypt before his introduction to Pharaoh and elevation to second in command. What were some of the biggest things happening in your life thirteen years ago?

3. Read Genesis 41:1–36. What are some words that describe Pharaoh's actions and attitudes in that passage? What are some words that describe Joseph?

4. Most Christians know we are supposed to "wait on the Lord." What does that mean to you? What does that look like on a day-to-day basis?

5. In what circumstances are you currently being forced to wait—especially to wait on God? How are you being affected by that waiting?

6. What are specific steps you can take this week to remain focused on God through prayer? What are specific steps you can take to rest in the reality that God is in control?

SIX

THE INTERSECTION
OF GOOD AND GOD

I remember the day as a sunny, summer Brazilian one. Denalyn and I were spending the afternoon with our friends Paul and Debbie. Their house was a welcome respite. We lived close to downtown Rio de Janeiro in a high-rise apartment. Paul and Debbie lived an hour away from the city center in a nice house where the air was cooler, the streets were cleaner, and life was calmer. Besides, they had a swimming pool.

Our two-year-old daughter, Jenna, loved to play with their kids. And that is exactly what she was doing when she fell. We didn't intend to leave the children unattended. We had stepped into the house for just a moment to fill our plates. We were chatting and chewing when Paul and Debbie's four-year-old walked into the room and casually told her mom, "Jenna fell in the pool." We exploded out the door. Jenna was flopping in the water, wearing neither floaties nor a life jacket. Paul reached her first. He jumped in and lifted her up to Denalyn. Jenna coughed and cried for a minute, and just like that she was fine. Tragedy averted. Daughter safe.

Imagine our gratitude. We immediately circled up the kids, offered a prayer, and sang a song of thanks. For the remainder of the day, our feet didn't touch the ground, and Jenna didn't leave our arms. Even driving home, I was thanking God. In the rearview mirror I could see Jenna sound asleep in her car seat, and I offered yet another prayer: *God, you are so good.* Then a question surfaced in my thoughts. From God? Or from the part of me that struggles to make sense out of God? I can't say. But what the voice asked, I still remember: *If Jenna hadn't survived, would God still be good?*

I had spent the better part of the afternoon broadcasting God's goodness. Yet had we lost Jenna, would I have reached a different verdict? Is God good only when the outcome is?

When the cancer is in remission, we say, "God is good." When the pay raise comes, we announce, "God is good." When the university admits us or the final score favors our team, "God is good." Would we and do we say the same under different circumstances? In the cemetery as well as the nursery? In the unemployment line as well as the grocery line? In days of recession as much as in days of provision? Is God always good?

Most, if not all of us, have a contractual agreement with God. The fact that he hasn't signed it doesn't keep us from believing it.

I pledge to be a good, decent person, and in return God will . . .
save my child.
heal my wife.
protect my job.
(fill in the blank) _____

_____.

Only fair, right? Yet when God fails to meet our bottom-line expectations, we are left spinning in a tornado of questions. Is he good at all? Is God angry at me? Stumped? Overworked? Is his power limited? His authority restricted? Did the devil outwit him? When life isn't good, what are we to think about God? Where is he in all this?

Joseph's words for Pharaoh offer some help here. We don't typically think of Joseph as a theologian. Not like

Job the sufferer or Paul the apostle. For one thing, we don't have many of Joseph's words. Yet the few we have reveal a man who wrestled with the nature of God.

To the king he announced,

> But afterward there will be seven years of famine so great that all the prosperity will be forgotten in Egypt. Famine will destroy the land. This famine will be so severe that even the memory of the good years will be erased. As for having two similar dreams, it means that these events have been decreed by God, and he will soon make them happen. (Gen. 41:30–32 NLT)

Joseph saw both seasons, the one of plenty and the one of paucity, beneath the umbrella of God's jurisdiction. Both were "decreed by God."

How could this be? Was the calamity God's idea?

Of course not. God never creates or parlays evil. "God can never do wrong! It is impossible for the Almighty to do evil" (Job 34:10 NCV; James 1:17). He is the essence of good. How can he who is good invent anything bad?

And he is sovereign. Scripture repeatedly attributes utter and absolute control to his hand. "The Most High

God rules the kingdom of mankind and sets over it whom he will" (Dan. 5:21 ESV).

God is good. God is sovereign. Then how are we to factor in the presence of calamities in God's world?

Here is how the Bible does it: God permits it. When the demons begged Jesus to send them into a herd of pigs, he "gave them permission" (Mark 5:13). Regarding the rebellious, God said, "I defiled them . . . that I might fill them with horror so they would know that I am the LORD" (Ezek. 20:26 NIV). The law of Moses speaks of the consequence of accidentally killing a person: "If it is not done intentionally, but God lets it happen, they are to flee to a place I will designate" (Ex. 21:13 NIV).

God at times permits tragedies. He permits the ground to grow dry and stalks to grow bare. He allows Satan to unleash mayhem. But he doesn't allow Satan to triumph. That is the promise of Romans 8:28: "And we know that in all things God works for the good of those who love him, who have been called according to his purpose" (NIV). God promises to render beauty out of "all things," not "each thing." The isolated events may be evil, but the ultimate culmination is good.

We see small examples of this in our own lives. When you sip on a cup of coffee and say, "This is good," what are you saying? The plastic bag that contains the beans is good? The beans themselves are good? Hot water is good? A coffee filter is good? No, none of these. *Good* happens when the ingredients work together: the bag opened, the beans ground, the water heated to the right temperature. It is the collective cooperation of the elements that creates good.

Nothing in the Bible would cause us to call a famine good or a heart attack good or a terrorist attack good. These are terrible calamities, born out of a fallen earth. Yet every message in the Bible, especially the story of Joseph, compels us to believe that God will mix them with other ingredients and bring good out of them.

But we must let God define *good*. Our definition includes health, comfort, and recognition. His definition? In the case of his Son, Jesus Christ, the good life consisted of struggles, storms, and death. But God worked it all together for the greatest of good: his glory and our salvation.

Joni Eareckson Tada has spent most of her life attempting to reconcile the presence of suffering with the nature of God. She was just a teenager when a diving accident left her paralyzed from the neck down. After more than forty years in a wheelchair, Joni reached this conclusion:

[Initially] I figured that if Satan and God were involved in my accident at all, then it must be that the devil had twisted God's arm for permission. . . .

I reasoned that once God granted permission to Satan, he then nervously had to run behind him with a repair kit, patching up what Satan had ruined, mumbling to himself, "Oh great, now how am I going to work this for good?" . . .

But the truth is that God is infinitely more powerful than Satan. . . .

While the devil's motive in my disability was to shipwreck my faith by throwing a wheelchair in my way, I'm convinced that God's motive was to thwart the devil and use the wheelchair to change me and make me more like Christ through it all. . . .

[He can] bring ultimate good out of the devil's wickedness.[12]

This was the message of Jesus. When his followers spotted a blind man on the side of the road, they asked Jesus for an explanation. Was God angry? Who was to blame? Who sinned? Jesus' answer provided a higher option: The man was blind so "the works of God should be revealed in him" (John 9:3). God turned blindness, a bad thing, into a billboard for Jesus' power to heal. Satan acted, God counteracted, and good won. It's a divine jujitsu of sorts. God redirects the energy of evil against its source. God "uses evil to bring evil to naught."[13] He is the master chess player, always checkmating the devil's moves.

Our choice comes down to this: Trust God or turn away. He will cross the line. He will shatter our expectations. And we will be left to make a decision.

At some point we all stand at this intersection: Is God good when the outcome is not? During the famine as well as the feast? The definitive answer comes in the person of Jesus Christ. He is the only picture of God ever taken. Do you want to know heaven's clearest answer to the question of suffering? Look at Jesus.

He pressed his fingers into the sore of the leper. He felt the tears of the sinful woman who wept. He inclined his ear to the cry of the hungry. He wept at the death of a friend. He stopped his work to tend to the needs of a grieving mother. He doesn't recoil, run, or retreat at the sight of pain. Just the opposite. He didn't walk the earth in an insulated bubble or preach from an isolated, germ-free, pain-free island. He took his own medicine. He played by his own rules. Trivial irritations of family life? Jesus felt them. Cruel accusations of jealous men? Jesus knew their sting. A seemingly senseless death? Just look at the cross. He exacts nothing from us that he did not experience himself.

Why? Because he is good.

God owes us no more explanation than this. Besides, if he gave one, what makes us think we would understand it? Might the problem be less God's plan and more our limited perspective? Suppose the wife of George Frideric Handel came upon a page of her husband's famous oratorio *Messiah*. The entire work was more than two hundred pages long. Imagine that she discovered one page on the kitchen table. On it her husband had written only one measure in a minor key, one that didn't work on its own. Suppose she, armed with this fragment of dissonance, marched into his studio and said, "This music makes no sense. You are a lousy composer." What would he think?

> Because he is good, God exacts nothing from us that he did not experience himself.

Perhaps something similar to what God thinks when we do the same. We point to our minor key—our sick child, crutches, or cancer—and say, "This makes no sense!" Yet out of all his creation, how much have we seen? And of all his work how much do we understand? Only a sliver. A doorway peephole. Is it possible that some explanation for suffering exists of which we know nothing at all? What if God's answer to the question of suffering requires more megabytes than our puny minds have been given?

And is it possible that the wonder of heaven will make the most difficult life a good bargain? This was Paul's opinion. "Our light and momentary troubles are achieving for us an eternal glory that far outweighs them all" (2 Cor. 4:17 NIV).

Suppose I invited you to experience the day of your dreams. Twenty-four hours on an island paradise with your favorite people, food, and activities. The only stipulation: one millisecond of discomfort. For reasons I choose not to explain, you will need to begin the day with the millisecond of distress.

Would you accept my offer? I think you would. A split second is nothing compared to twenty-four hours. On God's clock you're in the middle of your millisecond. Compared to eternity, what is seventy, eighty, ninety years? Just a vapor. Just a finger snap compared to heaven.

Your pain won't last forever, but you will. "Whatever we may have to go through now is less than nothing compared with the magnificent future God has planned for us" (Rom. 8:18 PHILLIPS).

What is coming will make sense of what is happening

now. Let God finish his work. Let the composer complete his symphony. The forecast is simple. Good days. Bad days. But God is in *all* days. He is the Lord of the famine and the Lord of the feast, and he uses both to accomplish his will.

Therefore, take heart. Better yet, take hope.

—— REFLECTION QUESTIONS ——

1. Have you witnessed an example of faith under fire? How has it affected your own approach to struggle, pain, or loss?

2. It's easy for Christians to slip into "if-then" contracts with God. *If I do this, then God will. . . .* Why is that a problem?

3. Read Joseph's interpretations of Pharaoh's dreams in Genesis 41:25–36. What can we learn from those verses about God's nature and character?

4. Most of us know on an intellectual level that God is always good, but that knowledge can be tested by circumstances. When have you questioned God's goodness? His fairness?

5. When have you experienced the unadulterated goodness of God filling or uplifting your life? How did you respond?

6. We will mature in our faith when we can hope and trust in God regardless of whether our circumstances are good or bad. What obstacles are holding you back from that level of faith?

SEVEN

A DISH BEST UNSERVED

In 1882, a New York City businessman named Joseph Richardson owned a narrow strip of land on Lexington Avenue. It was 5 feet wide and 104 feet long. Another businessman, Hyman Sarner, owned a normal-sized lot adjacent to Richardson's skinny one. He wanted to build apartments that fronted the avenue. He offered Richardson $1,000 for the slender plot. Richardson was deeply offended by the amount and demanded $5,000. Sarner refused, and Richardson called Sarner a tightwad and slammed the door on him.

Sarner assumed the land would remain vacant and instructed the architect to design the apartment building with windows overlooking the avenue. When Richardson saw the finished building, he resolved to block the view. No one was going to enjoy a free view over his lot.

So seventy-year-old Richardson built a house. Five feet wide and 104 feet long and four stories high with two suites on each floor. Upon completion, he and his wife moved into one of the suites.

Only one person at a time could ascend the stairs or pass through the hallway. The largest dining table in any suite was eighteen inches wide. The stoves were the very smallest made. A newspaper reporter of some girth once got stuck in the stairwell, and after two tenants were unsuccessful in pushing him free, he exited only by stripping down to his undergarments.

The building was dubbed the "Spite House." Richardson spent the last fourteen years of his life in the narrow residence that seemed to fit his narrow state of mind.[14]

The Spite House was torn down in 1915, which is odd. I distinctly remember spending a few nights there last year. And a few weeks there some years back. If memory serves, didn't I see you squeezing through the hallway?

Revenge builds a lonely house. Space enough for one person. The lives of its tenants are reduced to one goal: make someone miserable. They do. Themselves.

No wonder God insists that we "keep a sharp eye out for weeds of bitter discontent. A thistle or two gone to seed can ruin a whole garden in no time" (Heb. 12:15 MSG).

His healing includes a move out of the house of spite, a shift away from the cramped world of grudge and toward spacious ways of grace, away from hardness and toward forgiveness. He moves us forward by healing our past.

Can he really? This mess? This history of sexual abuse? This raw anger at the father who left my mother? This seething disgust I feel every time I think of the one who treated me like yesterday's trash? Can God heal this ancient hurt in my heart?

Joseph asked these questions. You never outlive the memory of ten brothers giving you the heave-ho, but Joseph tried to bury it. By the time he saw his brothers again, he'd been prime minister for nearly a decade. He wore a chain of gold on his neck. He bore the king's seal on his hand. The blood-bedabbled coat of colors had been replaced with the royal robe of the king. The kid from Canaan had come a long way.

Joseph could travel anywhere he wanted, yet he chose not to return to Canaan. Assemble an army and settle the score with his brothers? He had the resources. Send for his father? Or at least send a message? He'd had perhaps eight years to set the record straight. He knew where to find his family, but he chose not to contact them. He kept family secrets a secret. Untouched and untreated.

He was content to leave his past in the past.

But God was not. Restoration matters to God. The healing of the heart involves the healing of the past. So God shook things up.

"All countries came to Joseph in Egypt to buy grain, because the famine was severe in all lands" (Gen. 41:57). And in the long line of folks appealing for an Egyptian handout, look what the cat dragged in. "Joseph's ten brothers went down to buy grain in Egypt" (42:3).

> Restoration matters to God. The healing of the heart involves the healing of the past.

Joseph heard them before he saw them. He was fielding a question from a servant when he detected the Hebrew chatter. Not just the language of his heart but the dialect of his home. The prince motioned for the servant to stop speaking. He turned and looked. There they stood.

The brothers were balder, grayer, rough skinned. They were pale and gaunt with hunger. Sweaty robes clung to their shins, and road dust chalked their cheeks. These Hebrews stuck out in sophisticated Egypt like hill-billies at Times Square. When their time came to ask Joseph for grain, they didn't recognize him. His beard was shaved, his robe was royal, and the language he spoke was Egyptian. Black makeup extended from the sides of his eyes. He wore a black wig that sat on his head like a helmet. It never occurred to them that they were standing before their baby brother.

Their baby brother's response was . . . strange. He spoke to them gruffly; even harshly. He accused them of being spies. When they protested their innocence and spoke about their family, he refused to hear. He made odd demands of his brothers:

> "In this manner you shall be tested: By the life of Pharaoh, you shall not leave this place unless your youngest brother comes here. Send one of you, and let him bring your brother; and you shall be kept in prison, that your words may be tested to see whether there is any truth in you; or else, by the life of Pharaoh, surely you are spies!" So he put them all together in prison three days. (Gen. 42:15–17)

By the third day of their imprisonment, Joseph relented. A little. He spoke with a snarl:

> "Do this and live, for I fear God. If you are honest men, let one of your brothers be confined to your

prison house; but you, go and carry grain for the famine of your houses. And bring your youngest brother to me; so your words will be verified, and you shall not die." (Gen. 42:18–20)

Joseph gave them a taste of their own medicine. "Take that, you rascals!"

Isn't it good to know that Joseph was human? The guy was so good it hurt. He endured slavery, succeeded in a foreign land, mastered a new language, and resisted sexual seductions. He was the model prisoner and the perfect counselor to the king. Scratch him, and he bled holy blood. We expect him to see his brothers and declare, "Father, forgive them, for they knew not what they did" (Luke 23:34). But he didn't. He didn't because forgiving jerks is the hardest trick in the bag. We will feed the poor and counsel the king. Why, we'll memorize the book of Leviticus if God says to do so.

But . . .

"Don't let the sun go down while you are still angry" (Eph. 4:26 NLT).

"Let all bitterness, wrath, anger, clamor, and evil speaking be put away from you, with all malice" (Eph. 4:31).

"As Christ forgave you, so you also must do" (Col. 3:13).

Really, God?

I have a friend who was six years old when her mother ran off with a salesman, leaving her to be raised by a good-hearted dad who knew nothing about dolls, dresses, or dates. The father and daughter stumbled through life and made the best of it. Recently the mom reappeared, like a brother out of Canaan; she requested a coffee date with my friend, and said, "I'm sorry for abandoning you." The mom wants to reenter her daughter's world.

My friend's first thought was, *That's it? I'm supposed to forgive you?* Seems too easy. Doesn't the mom need to experience what she gave? A few years wondering if she will see her daughter again. Some pain-filled nights. A bit of justice. How do we reconcile the pain of the daughter with God's command to forgive? Isn't some vengeance in order?

Of course it is. In fact, God cares about justice more than we do. Paul admonished, "Never pay back evil for evil. . . . Never avenge yourselves. Leave that to God, for he has said that he will repay those who deserve it" (Rom. 12:17, 19 TLB).

We fear the evildoer will slip into the night, unknown and unpunished. Escape to Fiji and sip mai tais on the beach. Not to worry. Scripture says, "[God] *will* repay," not he "*might* repay." God will execute justice on behalf of truth and fairness. Case in point? Prepare yourself for the most surprising turnaround of the Joseph story.

After three days Joseph released all but one brother from jail. They returned to Canaan to report to Jacob, their father, a weak shadow of an old man. The brothers told him how Simeon was kept in Egypt as assurance they would return with Benjamin, the youngest brother. Jacob had nothing to say except, "You have bereaved me: Joseph is no more, Simeon is no more, and you want to take Benjamin. All these things are against me" (Gen. 42:36).

Such a louse. Jacob played favorites, refused to discipline, had multiple wives, and upon hearing of the imprisonment of his son, had a pity party. What a prima donna. No wonder the family was screwed up.

But as we read further, a light breaks through the clouds. Judah, who once wanted to get rid of Joseph, stepped forward. "Send [Benjamin] with me, and we will arise and go, that we may live and not die, both we and you and also our little ones. I myself will be surety for him; from my hand you shall require him. If I do not bring him back to you and set him before you, then let me bear the blame forever" (Gen. 43:8–9).

Is this the same Judah? The same man who said,

"Let us sell him to the Ishmaelites" (37:27)? The same brother who helped negotiate the slave trade?

Well, yes . . . and no.

Judah, as it turns out, has had his own descent into the pit. After Joseph's abduction Judah went on to have three sons. He arranged for the eldest to marry a girl named Tamar. But the son died. Following the proper protocol of his day, Judah arranged for his second son to marry Tamar. The son didn't manage the situation well and died. Judah assumed Tamar was jinxed. Afraid that his third son would meet the same fate, Judah put the matter on hold, leaving Tamar with no husband.

Later Judah's wife died. Tamar heard that Judah was coming to town. Apparently she hadn't been able to get Judah to reply to her emails, so she got creative. She disguised herself as a prostitute and made him an offer. Judah took the bait. He exchanged his necklace and walking stick for sex, unaware that he was sleeping with his daughter-in-law. (Oh, how lust blinds a man!) She conceived. Three months later she reappeared in Judah's life as Tamar, *pregnant* Tamar. Judah went high and mighty on her and demanded she be burned. That's when she produced Judah's necklace and walking stick, and Judah realized the child was his. He was caught in his own sin, disgraced in front of his own family.

Things had come full circle. Judah, who had deceived Jacob, was deceived. Judah, who had trapped Joseph, was trapped. Judah, who had helped humiliate Joseph, was humiliated. God gave Judah his comeuppance, and Judah came to his senses. "She has been more righteous than I," he confessed (Gen. 38:26).

For years I wondered why Judah's exploits were included in the Joseph narrative. They interrupt everything. We just get started in chapter 37 with the dreams and drama of Joseph when the narrator dedicates chapter 38 to the story of Judah, the hustler, and Tamar, the faux escort. Two dead husbands. One clever widow. An odd, seemingly poorly placed story. But now I see how it fits.

For anything good to happen to Jacob's family, someone in the clan had to grow up. If not the father, one of the brothers had to mature to the point where he took responsibility for his actions. God activated the change in Judah. He gave the guy a taste of his own medicine, and the medicine worked! Judah championed the family cause. He spoke sense into his father's head. He was willing to take responsibility for Benjamin's safety and bear the blame if he failed. Judah got his wake-up call, and Joseph didn't have to lift a finger or swing a fist.

Vengeance *is* God's. He *will* repay—whether ultimately on the Day of Judgment or intermediately in this life. The point of the story? God handles all Judahs. He can discipline your abusive boss, soften your angry parent. He can bring your ex to his knees or to her senses. Forgiveness doesn't diminish justice; it just entrusts it to God. He guarantees the right retribution. We give too much or too little. But the God of justice has the precise prescription.

Unlike us, God never gives up on a person. Never. Long after we have moved on, God is still there, probing the conscience, stirring conviction, always orchestrating redemption. Fix your enemies? That's God's job.

Forgive your enemies? Ah, that's where you and I come in. We forgive. "Do not let the sun go down on your anger, and do not give the devil an opportunity" (Eph. 4:26–27 NASB). The word translated *opportunity* is the Greek word *topos*,[15] the same term from which we get the English noun *topography*. It means territory or ground. Interesting. Anger gives ground to the devil. Bitterness invites him to occupy a space in your heart, to rent a room. Believe me, he will move in and stink up the place. Gossip, slander, temper—anytime you see these, Satan has claimed a bunk.

> Forgiveness doesn't diminish justice; it just entrusts it to God.

Evict him. Don't even give him the time of day. In the name of Jesus tell him to pack his bags and hit the road.

Begin the process of forgiveness. Keep no list of wrongs. Pray for your antagonists rather than plot against them. Hate the wrong without hating wrongdoers. Turn your attention away from what they did *to* you to what Jesus did *for* you. Outrageous as it may seem, Jesus died for them too. If he thinks they are worth forgiving, they are. Does that make forgiveness easy? No. Quick? Seldom. Painless? It wasn't for Joseph.

The brothers returned to Egypt from Canaan, Benjamin in tow. Joseph invited them to a dinner. He asked about Jacob, spotted Benjamin, and all but came undone. "God be gracious to you, my son," he blurted before he hurried out of the room to weep (Gen. 43:29).

He returned to eat and drink and make merry with his brothers. Joseph sat them according to birth order. He singled out Benjamin for special treatment. Every time the brothers got one helping, Benjamin got five. They noticed this. But said nothing.

Joseph loaded their sacks with food and hid his personal cup in Benjamin's sack. The brothers were barely down the road when Joseph's steward stopped their caravan, searched their sacks, and found the cup. The brothers tore their clothes (the ancient equivalent of pulling out one's hair) and soon found themselves back in front of Joseph, fearing for their lives.

Joseph couldn't make up his mind! He welcomed them, wept over them, ate with them, and then played a trick on them. He was at war with himself. These brothers had peeled the scab off his oldest and deepest wound. And he would be hanged before he'd let them do it again. On the other hand, these were his brothers, and he would be hanged before he lost them again.

Forgiveness vacillates like this. It has fits and starts, good days and bad. Anger intermingled with love. Irregular mercy. We make progress only to make a wrong turn. Step forward and fall back. But this is okay. When it comes to forgiveness, all of us are beginners. No one owns a secret formula. As long as you are trying to forgive, you are forgiving. It's when you no longer try that bitterness sets in.

So, don't give up. Keep hold of hope. Stay the course.

You'll spend less time in the spite house and more in the grace house. And as one who has walked the hallways of both, I can guarantee that you are going to love the space of grace.

── **REFLECTION QUESTIONS** ──

1. What did you find surprising in this chapter? What did you find confusing?

2. What do you think about how Joseph handled the situation with his brothers? Do you typically express your desire for revenge in active ways or passive ways? What is one example that comes to mind?

3. Read Genesis 42:1–24. What are some words that describe Joseph in that passage? What are some words that describe his brothers?

4. Ephesians 4:31 says, "Let all bitterness, wrath, anger, clamor, and evil speaking be put away from you, with all malice." What would it look like to obey that command in full? What impact would doing so have on your life?

5. There are few tasks in life more difficult than forgiving those who have wronged us in major ways. When have you experienced a moment of forgiveness that shook you or shocked you?

6. Describe a situation in which you have an opportunity to forgive someone right now. What's holding you back?

EIGHT

HE AIN'T HEAVY, HE'S MY BROTHER

You've never seen a scene like this. The basketball player stands at the free throw line. His team is down by one point. Only a few seconds remain on the game clock. Players on both teams crouch, ready to grab the rebound. The shooter positions the ball in his hand. The crowd is quiet. The cheerleaders gulp. Again, you've never seen a scene like this. How can I be so sure? Because the player shooting the ball has never seen a scene like this.

He's blind.

Everyone else on his team is sighted. Everyone on the other team is sighted. But Matt Steven, a high school senior in Upper Darby, Pennsylvania, can't see a thing. His brother stands under the rim, rapping a cane on the basket. Matt listens, dribbles, and lifts the ball to shoot. We wonder, Why does a basketball coach place a blind kid on the foul line?

The short answer? Because he is Matt's big brother.

The long answer began years earlier when Matt was born with two permanently detached retinas. He lost his left eye in the fifth grade and his right eye in the sixth. But even though Matt can't see, his big brother has enough vision for them both. Joe spent a childhood helping Matt do the impossible: ride a bike, ice-skate, and play soccer. So when Joe began coaching the basketball team, he brought his baby brother with him as the equipment manager. Matt never practices or plays with the team. But with Joe's help he shoots free throws after every practice. Long after the team leaves, the brothers linger—the younger one at the charity line, the older one beneath the basket, tapping a stick against the rim.

And so it is that Matt, for this tournament game, is the designated free throw shooter. Joe convinced the refs and the opponents to let Matt play. Everyone thought it was a great idea. But no one imagined the game would come down to this shot.

So far Matt is 0 for 6. The gym falls silent. Joe hits the steel rim of the basket with the cane. Up in the stands Matt's mom tries to steady the video camera.

Matt dribbles. Pauses and shoots. Swish! The game is tied! The screams of the fans lift the roof of the gymnasium. Finally the crowd settles down so Matt can hear the click, and the scene-never-seen repeats itself. Swish number two! The opposing team grabs the ball and throws a Hail Mary at the other basket and misses. The game is over, and Matt is the hero. Everyone whoops and hollers while Matt—the hero—tries to find his way to the bench. Guess who comes to help him. You got it. Joe.[16]

Big brothers can make all the difference. Got bullies on your block? Big brother can protect you. Forgot your lunch money? Big brother has some extra. Can't keep your balance on your bike? He'll steady you. Call your big brother.

Big brother. Bigger than you. Stronger. Wiser.

Big *brother.* Since he is family, you are his priority. He has one job: to get you through things. Through the neighborhood without getting lost, through the math quiz without failing, through the shopping mall without stopping. Big brothers walk us through the rough patches of life.

Need one? You aren't trying to make a basket, but you are trying to make a living or make a friend or make sense out of the bad breaks you've been getting. Could you use the protection of a strong sibling?

The sons of Jacob certainly needed it. As they stood before Joseph, they were the picture of pity. Accused of stealing the silver cup. Tongue-tied goat herders before a superpower sovereign. Nothing to offer but prayers, nothing to request but help. Judah told the prince their story. How their father was frail and old. How one son had perished and how also losing Benjamin would surely kill their father. Judah even offered to stay in Benjamin's place if that was what it would take to save his family. They were face-first on the floor, hoping for mercy, but they received much more.

Joseph told the officials to clear out, his translators to leave the room. "Then Joseph could not restrain himself" (Gen. 45:1). He buried his face in his hands and began to heave with emotion. He didn't weep gently or whimper softly. He wailed. The cries echoed in the palace hallways, cathartic moans of a man in a moment of deep healing. Twenty-two years of tears and trickery had come to an end. Anger and love had dueled it out. Love won.

He broke the news: "I am Joseph; does my father still live?" (v. 3). Eleven throats gulped, and twenty-two eyes widened to the size of saucers. The brothers, still in a deep genuflect, dared not move. They ventured glances at each other and mouthed the name: *Joseph?* Their last memory of their younger brother was of a pale-faced, frightened lad being carted off to Egypt. They had counted their coins and washed their hands of the boy. He was a teenager then. He was a prince now? They lifted their heads ever so slightly.

Joseph lowered his hands. His makeup was tear smeared, and his chin still quivered. His voice shook as he spoke. "Please come near to me." They rose to their feet. Slowly. Cautiously. "I am Joseph your brother, whom you sold into Egypt" (v. 4).

Joseph told them not to fear. "God sent me here. God did this. God is protecting you" (v. 7). In today's language, "There's more to our story than meets the eye."

The brothers were still not sure who this man was. This man who wept for them, called for them . . . and then cared for them.

Fetch your family, he instructed, and come to Egypt. He promised to provide for them and sealed the promise with even more tears. He stood from his chair and threw his arms around his baby brother. "He fell on his brother Benjamin's neck and wept. . . . He kissed all his brothers and wept over them, and after that his brothers talked with him" (vv. 14–15).

One by one he received them. Judah, the one who came up with the slave trafficking idea. Reuben, the firstborn who didn't always behave like a big brother. Simeon and Levi, who wrought such violence at Shechem that their father deemed them "instruments of cruelty" (Gen. 49:5).[17] Those who had tied Joseph's hands and mocked his cries. He kissed them all.

Hostility and anger melted onto the marble floor. Joseph didn't talk at them or over them. They just talked. "How's Dad? Reuben, you're looking chubby. Simeon, how's your health? Levi, did you ever marry that girl from across the field? Have any kids? Any grandkids?"

When Pharaoh heard about Joseph's siblings, Pharaoh told him, "Any family of yours is a family of mine." And the next thing you know, Joseph was outfitting his brothers in new clothes and carts. They were honorary citizens of Egypt. Outcasts one moment. People of privilege the next.

At about this point the brothers began to realize they were out of danger. The famine still raged. The fields still begged. Circumstances were still hostile. But they were finally safe. They would make it through this. Because they were good men? No, because they were family. The prince was their brother.

Oh, for such a gift. We know the feel of a famine. Like the brothers of Joseph, we've found ourselves in dry seasons. Resources gone. Supplies depleted. Energy expired. We've stood where the brothers stood.

We've done what the brothers did. We've hurt the people we love. Sold them into slavery? Maybe not. But lost our temper? Misplaced our priorities? You bet. Like the shepherds of Beersheba, we've sought help from the Prince, our Prince. We've offered our prayers and pleaded our cases. We've wondered if he would have a place for the likes of us. What the brothers found in Joseph's court, we find in Jesus Christ. The Prince is our brother.

Is this a new thought for you? You've heard Jesus described as King, Savior, and Lord, but Brother? This is biblical language. On one occasion Jesus was speaking to his followers when his family tried to get his attention. His mother and brothers stood outside and sent word that they wanted to speak to him. Jesus took advantage of the moment to make a tender gesture and statement. "He stretched out His hand toward His disciples and said, 'Here are My mother and My brothers! For whoever does the will of My Father in heaven is My brother and sister and mother'" (Matt. 12:49–50).

Had you and I been present that day, we would have looked at the "family" of Jesus and seen little to impress us. None of his followers was of noble birth. No deep pockets or blue blood. Peter had his swagger. John had his temper. Matthew had his checkered past and colorful friends. Like Jacob's sons in the Egyptian court, they seemed outclassed and out of place. Yet Jesus was not embarrassed to call them his family. He laid claim to them in public.

He lays claim to us as well. "Jesus, who makes people holy, and those who are made holy are from the same family. So he is not ashamed to call them his brothers and sisters" (Heb. 2:11 NCV).

Jesus redefined his family to include all who come near him.

The account of Joseph is simply an appetizer for the Bible's main course, the story of Jesus. So many similarities exist between the two men. Joseph was the favorite son of Jacob. Jesus was the beloved Son of God (Matt. 3:17). Joseph wore the coat of many colors. Jesus did the deeds of many wonders. Joseph fed the nations. Jesus fed the multitudes. Joseph prepared his people for the coming famine. Jesus came to prepare his people for eternity. Under Joseph's administration grain increased. In the hands of Jesus, hands water became the finest wine, and a basket of bread became a buffet for thousands. Joseph responded to

> Jesus redefined his family to include all who come near him.

a crisis of nature. Jesus responded to one crisis after another. He told typhoons to settle down and waves to be quiet. He commanded cadavers to stand up, the crippled to dance a jig, and the mute to sing an anthem.

And people hated him for it.

Joseph was sold for twenty pieces of silver, Jesus for thirty. Joseph was falsely accused and thrown into a prison. Jesus was condemned for no cause and nailed to a cross. The brothers thought they had seen the last of Joseph. The soldiers sealed the tomb, thinking the same about Jesus. But Joseph resurfaced as a prince. So did Jesus. While his killers slept and followers wept, Jesus stood up from the slab of death. He unwrapped his burial clothes and stepped out into the Sunday morning sunrise.

God gave Jesus what Pharaoh gave Joseph: a promotion to the highest place.

> God raised him from death and set him on a throne in deep heaven, in charge of running the universe, everything from galaxies to governments, no name and no power exempt from his rule. And not just for the time being, but *forever*. He is in charge of it all, has the final word on everything. (Eph. 1:20–22 MSG)

This is where the similarities cease. Joseph's reign and life eventually ended. But Jesus? Heaven will never see an empty throne. Jesus occupies it at this very moment. He creates weather patterns, redirects calendars, and recycles calamities—all with the goal of creating moments like this one in which we, his undeserving family, can hear him say, "I am Jesus, your Brother."

He weeps at the very sight of you. Not tears of shame but tears of joy.

He calls for you. "Come to me, all of you who are weary and carry heavy burdens, and I will give you rest" (Matt. 11:28 NLT). One foot of distance is too much. He wants us to come near. All of us. We who threw him into the pit. We who sold him out for silver. We who buried the very memory of our deeds. *Come. Come. Come.*

He cares for you. Joseph spoke to his king, and Jesus speaks to ours. In him "we have an Advocate with the Father, Jesus Christ the righteous" (1 John 2:1). Joseph gave his brothers wagons and robes. Your Brother promises to "supply all your need according to His riches" (Phil. 4:19).

Let's trust him to take care of us. Let's place our hope in him.

After Matt Steven made the foul shots, he became the hero of his high school. Everyone wanted to meet him. Cheerleaders wanted to talk to him. It was reported that he was thinking about asking a girl to the prom. Wonderful things happen when a big brother helps out.

You will get through this. Not because you are strong but because your Brother is. Not because you are good but because your Brother is. Not because you are big but because your big Brother is the Prince, and he has a place prepared for you.

REFLECTION QUESTIONS

1. What questions came to mind as you read through this chapter? Where can you go to find answers?

2. How did your siblings impact your life as you were growing up? How do they influence you now?

3. Read Genesis 45:1–28. What are the main emotions contained or expressed in that passage?

4. In what ways do you identify with Joseph as you read those verses? In what ways do you identify with his brothers?

5. How would you summarize your relationship with Jesus? In what ways are you connected with him? In what ways do you interact with him?

6. What obstacles get in the way of allowing Jesus to handle the problems in your life out of his strength and resources rather than your own?

NINE

A LONG-AWAITED
REUNION

John Glenn knew how to fly a fighter jet. He completed fifty-nine missions in World War II and ninety in the Korean War. He knew how to fly fast. He was the first pilot to average supersonic speed on a transcontinental flight. He knew how to fly into outer space. In 1962 he became the first American to orbit the earth.[18] John Glenn knew how to win elections. He was a United States senator from 1974 to 1999.

John Glenn could do much—give speeches, lead committees, inspire audiences, and write books. Yet for all his accomplishments, there is one skill he never mastered. He never learned to tell his wife goodbye.

The two met when they were toddlers and grew up

together in New Concord, Ohio. Though John went on to achieve national fame, he would tell you that the true hero of the family is the girl he married in 1943.

Annie suffered from such severe stuttering that 85 percent of her efforts to speak fell short. She couldn't talk on the phone, order food in a restaurant, or give verbal instructions to a taxi driver. The idea of requesting help in a department store intimidated her. She would wander the aisles, reluctant to speak. She feared the possibility of a family crisis because she didn't know if she could make a 911 call.

Hence the difficulty with *goodbye*. John couldn't bear the thought of separation. So the two developed a code. Each time he was deployed on a mission or called to travel, the couple bid each other farewell the same way. "I'm just going down to the corner store to get a pack of gum," he would say. "Don't be long," she'd reply. And off he would go to Japan, Korea, or outer space.

Over the years Annie's speech improved. Intense therapy clarified her enunciation skills and improved her confidence. Even so, *goodbye* was the one word the couple could not say to each other. In 1998, Senator Glenn became the oldest astronaut in history. He reentered space aboard the shuttle *Discovery*. Upon departure he told his wife, "I'm just going down to the corner store to get a pack of gum." This time he gave her a present: a pack of gum. She kept it in a pocket near her heart until he was safely home.[19]

Goodbye. No one wants to say it. Not the spouse of an astronaut. Not the mom of a soon-to-be preschooler. Not the father of the bride. Not the husband in the convalescent home. Not the wife in the funeral home.

Death is the interloper, the intruder, the stick-figure sketch in the Louvre. It doesn't fit. Why would God give a fishing buddy and then take him? Fill a crib and then empty it? No matter how you frame it, *goodbye* doesn't feel right.

Jacob and Joseph lived beneath the shadow of *goodbye.* When the brothers lied about Joseph's death, they gave Jacob a blood-soaked tunic. A wild beast dragged the body away, they implied. Jacob collapsed in sorrow. "Then Jacob tore his clothes, put on sackcloth and mourned for his son many days" (Gen. 37:34 NIV).

Jacob wept until the tears turned to brine, until his soul shriveled. The two people he loved the most were gone. Rachel dead. Joseph dead. Jacob, it seems, died. "All his sons and daughters came to comfort him, but he refused to be comforted. 'No,' he said, 'I will continue to mourn until I join my son in the grave.' So his father wept for him" (v. 35 NIV).

In just about all the ways that counted, Jacob had given up.

Joseph lived with the same sorrow. Two decades passed. No word from home. Birthdays, holidays, harvest days. Jacob was never far from his thoughts.

The moment Joseph revealed his identity to his brothers, he asked, "I am Joseph; does my father still live?" (Gen. 45:3).

Question number one: "How's Dad?" Priority number one: a family reunion. Joseph told his brothers to saddle up, ship out, and come back with the entire family.

He gave them supplies for the journey. And he gave each of them new clothes—but to Benjamin he gave five changes of clothes and 300 pieces of silver. He also sent his father ten male donkeys loaded with the finest products of Egypt, and ten female donkeys loaded with grain and bread and other supplies he would need on his journey. So Joseph sent his brothers off, and as they left, he called after them, "Don't quarrel about all this along the way!" And they left Egypt and returned to their father, Jacob, in the land of Canaan. (vv. 21–25 NLT)

Jacob's boys returned to Canaan in style. Gone were

the shabby robes and emaciated donkeys. They drove brand-new pickup trucks packed with gifts. They wore leather jackets and alligator skin boots. Their wives and kids spotted them on the horizon. "You're back! You're back!" Hugs and backslaps all around.

Jacob emerged from a tent. A rush of hair, long and silver, reached his shoulders. Stooped back. Face leathery, like rawhide. He squinted at the sun-kissed sight of his sons and all the plunder. He was just about to ask where they stole the stuff when one of them blurted, "'Joseph is still alive, and he is governor over all the land of Egypt.' And Jacob's heart stood still, because he did not believe them" (Gen. 45:26).

The old man grabbed his chest. He had to sit down. Leah brought him some water and glared at the sons as if to say they had better not be playing a joke on their father. But this was no trick. "When they told him all the words which Joseph had said to them, and when he saw the carts which Joseph had sent to carry him, the spirit of Jacob their father revived" (v. 27).

Sadness had sapped the last drop of joy out of Jacob. Yet when the sons told him what Joseph had said, how he had asked about Jacob, how he had called them to Egypt, Jacob's spirit revived. He looked at the prima facie evidence of carts and clothes. He looked at the confirming smiles and nods of his sons, and for the first time in more than twenty years, the old patriarch began to believe he would see his son again.

His eyes began to sparkle, and his shoulders straightened. "Then Israel said, 'It is enough. Joseph my son is still alive. I will go and see him before I die'" (Gen. 45:28). Yes, the narrator calls Jacob by his other name (given by God in Gen. 32:28). The promise of a family reunion can do this. It changes us. From sad to seeking. From lonely to longing. From hermit to pilgrim. From Jacob (the heel grabber) to Israel (prince of God).

"So Israel took his journey with all that he had, and came to Beersheba, and offered sacrifices to the God of his father Isaac" (Gen. 46:1). Jacob was 130 years old by this point. Hardly a spring chicken. He had a hitch in his "getalong," an ache in his joints. But nothing was going to keep him from his son. He took his staff in hand and issued the command: "Load 'em up! We are headed to Egypt."

As the entourage drew near, Jacob leaned forward to get a better glimpse of the man in the center chariot. When he saw his face, Jacob whispered, "Joseph, my son."

Across the distance Joseph leaned forward in his chariot. He told his driver to slap the horse. When the two groups met on the flat of the plain, the prince didn't hesitate. He bounded out of his chariot and ran in the direction of his father. "The moment Joseph saw him, he threw himself on his neck and wept" (Gen. 46:29 MSG).

Gone were the formalities. Forgotten were the proprieties. Joseph buried his face in the crook of his father's shoulder. "He wept a long time" (v. 29 MSG). As tears moistened the robe of his father, both men resolved that they would never say goodbye to each other again.

Goodbye. For some of you this word is the challenge of your life. To get through this is to get through raging loneliness, strength-draining grief. You sleep alone in a double bed. You walk the hallways of a silent house. You catch yourself calling out his name or reaching for her hand. As with Jacob, the separation has exhausted your spirit. You feel quarantined, isolated. The rest of the world has moved on; you ache to do the same. But you can't; you can't say goodbye.

If you can't, take heart. God has served notice. All farewells are on the clock. They are filtering like grains of sand through an hourglass. If heaven's throne room has a calendar, one day is circled in red and highlighted in yellow. God has decreed a family reunion.

> God has served notice. All farewells are on the clock.

The Master himself will give the command. Archangel thunder! God's trumpet blast! He'll come down from heaven and the dead in Christ will rise—they'll go first. Then the rest of us who are still alive at the time will be caught up with them into the clouds to meet the Master. Oh, we'll be walking on air! And then there will be one huge family reunion with the Master. So reassure one another with these words. (1 Thess. 4:16–18 MSG)

This day will be no small day. It will be the Great Day. The archangel will inaugurate it with a trumpet blast. Thousands and thousands of angels will appear in the sky (Jude 14–15). Cemeteries and seas will give up their dead. "Christ . . . will appear a second time, not to deal with sin but to save those who are eagerly waiting for him" (Heb. 9:28 ESV).

His coming will be the only event witnessed by all humanity. "Every eye will see Him" (Rev. 1:7). Moses will be watching. Napoleon's head will turn. The eyes of Martin Luther and Christopher Columbus will widen. The wicked despot of Hades. The white-robed martyr of paradise. From Adam to the baby born as the trumpet blares, everyone will witness the moment.

Just as the book of Genesis lists the family of Jacob,

the Book of Life lists the family of God. He will call the name of every person who accepted his invitation. He will honor the request of those who refused him and dismiss them for eternity. Then he will bless the desire of those who accepted him and gather them for a family reunion.

What a reunion it will be. "He will wipe every tear from their eyes" (Rev. 21:4 NIV). His first action will be to rub a thumb across the cheek of every child as if to say, "There, there . . . no more tears." This long journey will come to an end. You will see him.

And you will see *them*. Isn't this our hope? "There will be one huge family reunion with the Master. So reassure one another with these words" (1 Thess. 4:17–18 MSG).

Steven Curtis Chapman and his wife, Mary Beth, are banking on this promise. In May 2008 their beautiful five-year-old daughter was killed in an automobile accident. Since Steven is an internationally known and beloved Christian singer, words of support and concern poured in from all over the globe. Letters, emails, phone calls. The Chapmans were deluged by messages of kindness. One conversation in particular gave Steven strength. Pastor Greg Laurie, who had lost a son in an auto accident, told Steven, "Remember, your future with Maria is infinitely greater than your past with her."[20]

Death seems to take so much. We bury not just a body but the wedding that never happened, the golden years we never knew. We bury dreams. But in heaven these dreams will come true. God has promised a "restoration of all things" (Acts 3:21 ASV). "All things" includes all relationships.

Your grandpa? Aunt? Your child? They are looking toward the day when God's family is back together. Shouldn't we do the same? "Since we are surrounded by such a huge crowd of witnesses . . . let us run with endurance the race that God has set before us" (Heb. 12:1 NLT).

High above us there is a crowd of witnesses. They are the Abrahams, Jacobs, and Josephs from all generations and nations. They have completed their own events and now witness the races of their spiritual, if not physical, descendants. *Listen carefully*, the passage compels, *and you will hear a multitude of God's children urging you on*. "Run!" they shout. "Run! You'll get through this!"

Our final home will hear no goodbyes. We will speak of the Good Book and remember good faith—but *goodbye*? Gone forever.

Let the promise change you. From sagging to seeking, from mournful to hopeful. From dwellers in the land of goodbye to a heaven of hellos. The Prince has decreed a homecoming. Let's take our staffs and travel in his direction.

—— REFLECTION QUESTIONS ——

1. What made you stop and think as you read this chapter?

2. We all encounter death and loss. How has death touched your life most deeply? How has it shaped who you are as a person?

3. What are some "goodbyes" you are still recovering from? Still grieving?

4. Read Genesis 46:1–27. What can we learn about Jacob from these verses? What can we learn about Joseph?

5. In a typical week, how often do you think about heaven or eternal life? What steps could you take to contemplate those realities more often?

6. Take a moment to consider Hebrews 12:1: "Therefore we also, since we are surrounded by so great a cloud of witnesses, let us lay

aside every weight, and the sin which so easily ensnares us, and let us run with endurance
the race that is set before us." Who is part of
that "cloud of witnesses" cheering you on from
heaven?

TEN

GOD'S JOB. YOUR JOB.

S ee the hole in the skyline?"

I leaned forward and followed the finger of the driver. He was a rotund guy named Frank. Neck too big for his collar, hands too thick to wrap around the steering wheel. He pointed through the windshield at the forest of buildings called Lower Manhattan.

"The towers used to sit right there."

He could tell I couldn't see the spot.

"See the hole to the left of the one with the spire? Three days ago that was the World Trade Center. I looked at it each day as I came over the bridge. It was a powerful sight. The first morning I entered the city and saw no towers, I called my wife and cried."

To reach the epicenter of activity, we drove through layers of inactivity. Empty ambulances lined the road. Loved ones mingled outside the Family Care Center, where the USNS *Comfort*, a hospital ship, sat docked. Everyone waited. But each passing second took with it a grain of hope.

Three checkpoints later we parked the car and walked the final half mile. A week earlier this road had been full of flannel suits, cell phones, and market quotes. But on this day the sidewalk was muddy, and the air was thick with smoke. I decided not to think about what I was inhaling.

I didn't expect the fires. In spite of the rain and truckloads of water, flames still danced. I didn't anticipate the adjoining damage. Neighboring buildings were devastated. Intact windows were rare. The next-door Marriott had been gutted by the cockpit of a jet. Any other day it would have made the cover of a magazine.

But most of all I didn't expect the numbness. Not theirs, not mine. A flank of yellow-suited firemen, some twelve or so in width, marched past us. The same number walked toward us. Shift change. Those coming were grim. Those leaving were more so, faces as steely as the beams that coffined their comrades.

My response wasn't any different. No tears. No lump in the throat. Just numbness. *Several thousand people are under there*, I told myself. Yet I just stared. The tragedy spoke a language I'd never studied. I half expected—and even more, wanted—to hear someone yell, "Quiet on the set!" and see actors run out of the ruins. But the cranes carried no cameras, just concrete.

Later that night I spoke with an officer who guarded the entrance to the Family Care Center. He was posted next to the plywood wall of photos—the wailing wall, of sorts—on which relatives had tacked pictures and hopes. I asked him to describe the expressions on the faces of the people who had come to look at the pictures.

"Blank," he said. "Blank."

"They don't cry?"

"They don't cry."

"And you, have you cried?"

"Not yet. I just push it in."

Disbelief, for many, was the drug of choice.

We can relate. Calamities can leave us off balance and confused.

Consider the crisis of Joseph's generation. "Now there was no bread in all the land; for the famine was very severe, so that the land of Egypt and the land of Canaan languished because of the famine" (Gen. 47:13).

During the time Joseph was struggling to reconcile with his brothers, he was also navigating a catastrophe. It had been two years since the last drop of rain. The sky was endlessly blue. The sun relentlessly hot. Animal carcasses littered the ground, and no hope appeared on the horizon. The land was a dust bowl. No rain meant no farming. No farming meant no food. When people appealed to Pharaoh for help, he said, "Go to Joseph; whatever he says to you, do" (Gen. 41:55).

Joseph faced a calamity on a global scale.

Yet contrast the description of the problem with the outcome. Years passed, and the people told Joseph, "You have saved our lives; let us find favor in the sight of my lord, and we will be Pharaoh's servants" (47:25).

The people remained calm. A society that was ripe for bedlam actually thanked the government rather than attacked it. Makes a person wonder if Joseph ever taught a course in crisis management. If he did, he included the words he told his brothers: "God sent me before you to preserve life. For these two years the famine has been in the land, and there are still five years in which there will be neither plowing nor harvesting. And God sent me before you" (45:5–7).

Joseph began and ended his crisis assessment with references to God. God preceded the famine. God would outlive the famine. God was all over the famine. "God . . . famine . . . God."

How would you describe your crisis?

"The economy . . . the economy . . . the economy . . . the economy."

"The divorce . . . divorce . . . divorce . . . divorce."

"Doctors . . . diagnoses . . . doctors . . . diagnoses."

Do you recite your woes more naturally than you do heaven's strength? If so, no wonder life is tough. You're assuming God isn't in this crisis.

He is. Even a famine was fair game for God's purpose.

I remember a memorable breakfast with a friend. Most of our talk revolved around the health of his fourteen-year-old son. Seven years before, a tumor had been found behind the boy's spleen. The discovery led to several months of strenuous prayer and chemotherapy. The son recovered. He played high school football, and the cancer clinic is a distant memory.

The discovery of the tumor was the part of the story I found fascinating. When the boy was seven years old, he was horsing around with his cousins. One of them accidentally kicked him in the stomach. Acute pain led to a hospital visit. An alert doctor requested a series of tests. And the tests led the surgeon to discover and remove the tumor. After the cancer was removed, the father asked the physician how long the tumor had been present. Although it was impossible to know with certainty, the form and size of the tumor indicated it was no more than two or three days old.

"So," I said, "God used a kick in the gut to get your boy into treatment."

God doesn't manufacture pain, but he certainly puts it to use. "God . . . is the blessed controller of all things" (1 Tim. 6:15 PHILLIPS). His ways are higher than ours (Isa. 55:9). His judgments are unsearchable, and his paths are beyond tracing out (Rom. 11:33). We can't always see what God is doing, but can't we assume he is up to something good? Joseph did. He assumed God was in the crisis.

Then he faced the crisis with a plan. He collected grain during the good years and redistributed it in the bad. When the people ran out of food, he gave it to them in exchange for money, livestock, and property. After he stabilized the economy, he gave the people a lesson in money management. "Give one-fifth to Pharaoh, and use the rest for farming and eating" (Gen. 47:24, author's paraphrase).

> God doesn't manufacture pain, but he certainly puts it to use.

The plan could fit on an index card. "Save for seven years. Distribute for seven years. Manage carefully." Could his response have been simpler?

Could it have been more boring?

Some flamboyance would have been nice. A little bit of the Red Sea opening, Jericho's walls tumbling, or was-dead Lazarus walking. A dramatic crisis requires a dramatic response, right? Not always.

We equate spirituality with high drama: Paul raising the dead, Peter healing the sick. Yet for every Paul and Peter, there are a dozen Josephs. Men and women blessed with skills of administration. Steady hands through whom God saves people. Joseph never raised the dead, but he kept people from dying. He never healed the sick, but he kept sickness from spreading. He made a plan and stuck with it. And because he did, the nation survived. He triumphed with a calm, methodical plan.

In the days leading up to the war with Germany, the British government commissioned a series of posters. The idea was to capture encouraging slogans on paper and distribute them about the country. Capital letters in a distinct typeface were used, and a simple two-color format was selected. The only graphic was the crown of King George VI.

The first poster was distributed in September 1939:

YOUR COURAGE
YOUR CHEERFULNESS
YOUR RESOLUTION
WILL BRING
US VICTORY

Soon thereafter a second poster was produced:

FREEDOM IS
IN PERIL
DEFEND IT
WITH ALL
YOUR MIGHT

These two posters appeared up and down the British countryside. On railroad platforms and in pubs, stores, and restaurants. They were everywhere. A third poster was created yet never distributed. More than 2.5 million copies were printed yet never seen until nearly sixty years later when a bookstore owner in northeast England discovered one in a box of old books he had purchased at an auction. It read:

KEEP CALM
AND
CARRY ON

The poster bore the same crown and style of the first two posters. It was never released to the public, however, but was held in reserve for an extreme crisis, such as invasion by Germany. The bookstore owner framed it and hung it on the wall. It became so popular that the bookstore began producing identical images of the original design on coffee mugs, postcards, and posters. Everyone, it seems, appreciated the reminder from another generation to keep calm and carry on.[21]

Of all the Bible heroes, Joseph is the one most likely to have hung a copy of that poster on his office wall. He indwelt the world of ledgers, flowcharts, end-of-the-year reports, tabulations, and calculations. Day after day. Month after month. Year after year. He kept a cool head and carried on.

You can do the same. You can't control the weather. You aren't in charge of the economy. You can't undo the hurricane or unwreck the car, but you can map out a strategy. Remember, God is in this crisis. Ask him to give you an index card–sized plan, two or three steps you can take today.

Seek counsel from someone who has faced a similar challenge. Ask friends to pray. Look for resources. Reach out to a support group. Most importantly, make a plan.

And make sure that plan is bursting with hope.

Let me conclude with a critical question: Do you believe no evil is beyond God's reach? That he can redeem every pit, including this one in which you find yourself?

What if Joseph had given up on God? Lord knows, he could have turned his back on heaven. At any point along his broken road, he could have turned sour and walked away. "No more. No more. I'm out."

You could give up on God as well. The cemetery of hope is overpopulated with sour souls who have settled for a small god. Don't be among them.

God sees a Joseph in you. Yes, you! You in the pit. You with your family full of flops and failures. You incarcerated in your own version of an Egyptian jail. God is speaking to you.

Your family needs a Joseph, a courier of grace in a day of anger and revenge. Your descendants need a Joseph, a sturdy link in the chain of faith. Your generation needs a Joseph. There is a famine out there. Will you harvest hope and distribute it to the people? Will you be a Joseph?

> The cemetery of hope is overpopulated with sour souls who have settled for a small god. Don't be among them.

Trust God. No, *really* trust him. He will get you through this. Will it be easy or quick? I hope so. But it seldom is. Yet God will make good out of this mess.

That's his job.

Yours is to never give up.

God's Job. Your Job.

— **REFLECTION QUESTIONS** —

1. What encouraged or uplifted you in this chapter? Why?

2. Read Genesis 47:13–26. What can we learn about Joseph's nature and character from these verses?

3. In what ways did Joseph function well as a leader? As a planner?

4. What are some words that describe how you typically respond or perform during a crisis? Where would you like to improve in your ability to handle stress and chaos?

5. What are some important principles you have learned or encountered while reading *Never Give Up*?

6. God's job is to run the world. Your job is to never give up—to never give up hope in him. What is one step you can take this week to build up the amount of hope in your tank?

SEVEN STATEMENTS OF STRENGTH: A WEEK OF DEVOTIONALS

Day 1–You'll Get Through This

She had a tremble to her—the inner tremble you could feel with just a hand on her shoulder. I saw her in a grocery store. Had not seen her in some months. I asked about her kids and husband, and when I did, her eyes watered, her chin quivered, and the story spilled out. He'd left her. After twenty years of marriage, three kids, and a dozen moves, gone. Traded her in for a younger model. She did her best to maintain her composure but couldn't. The produce aisle became a sanctuary of sorts. Right there between the tomatoes and the heads of lettuce, she wept. We prayed. Then I said, "You'll get through this. It won't be painless. It won't be quick. But

God will use this mess for good. In the meantime don't be foolish or naive. But don't despair either. With God's help you will get through this."

Audacious of me, right? How dare I say such words? Where did I get the nerve to speak such a promise into tragedy? In a pit, actually. A deep, dark pit with ten brothers glaring down. The story of Joseph is the proof in this particular pudding.

One element that makes tragedies so tragic is their suddenness. It's like we're driving along life's highway one moment, and the next we're over a cliff. Rushing downward. Hurtling helplessly toward what seems like a kind of death.

Trouble is, we don't see well when we're in pain. We don't hear well when the wounds are fresh. We don't think well when the anger is pulsing between our temples. All the more reason to lean in toward the One who sees all, hears all, and understands everything and everyone. All the more reason to bank your hope in heaven.

Tomorrow is real. Tomorrow is coming. Never give up. Because you really will get through this.

Now may the God of hope fill you with all joy and
peace in believing, that you may abound in hope by
the power of the Holy Spirit. (Rom. 15:13)

Heavenly Father,

I know in my head that you are in charge and tomorrow is coming, but I need to feel that reality in my heart. Please help me to keep going and never give up. Please fill me with all joy and peace. Please fill me with hope through the power of your Holy Spirit. Please help me to know in full faith that I will get through this.

In Jesus' name,
Amen

·················

Day 2–It Won't Be Painless
My friend had just been fired. His fault. He'd made stupid, inappropriate remarks at work. Crude, offensive statements. His boss kicked him out. Now he's a fifty-seven-year-old unemployed manager in a rotten economy. He feels terrible and sounds worse. Wife angry. Kids confused. He needed assurance, so I gave it: "You'll get through this. It won't be painless. It won't be quick. But God will use this mess for good. In the meantime don't be foolish or naive. But don't despair either. Never give up. With God's help you will get through this."

It's an understandable misapprehension of the

Christian life that many of us believe pain is proof we're going the wrong way. We think pain is proof we're on the wrong path. Understandable, yes. Accurate—no.

Pain is a part of life in a fallen world. More importantly, pain is often a part of God's plan. Not a mistake. Not a wrong turn. But exactly where we're supposed to be.

If that sounds crazy, think about what it would take to climb out of a pit. Think about the sharp grain of the stone as you cling to the wall. Jagged points of pressure on the balls of your feet. Busted roots digging and scratching against your skin. Tangling in your hair. Think about aching muscles and scraped knees.

Painful! Much easier to just lay back and rest. No pain there in the dry, soft sand. Just close your eyes and drift away. Right?

Wrong. Giving up often seems painless. But it's the way of death.

It was Winston Churchill who said, "If you're going through hell—*keep going!*" Don't give up. Don't stop just because it's painful. Choose the way of life, even if it hurts.

> *Therefore we do not lose heart. Even though our*
> *outward man is perishing, yet the inward man is*

being renewed day by day. For our light affliction,
which is but for a moment, is working for us a far
more exceeding and eternal weight of glory. (2 Cor.
4:16–17)

Heavenly Father,
I understand that following your plan will
sometimes lead me into painful situations and
circumstances. I'm not asking for any hurts or
harm, but I say yes to your will. I say yes to your
plan. And I say yes to your healing according to
your timing. I will never give up.

In Jesus' name,
Amen

•••••••••••••••••

Day 3–It Won't Be Quick
She's fresh out of high school, hoping to get into college
next month. Her life hasn't been easy. When she was six
years old, her parents divorced. When she was fifteen,
they remarried, only to divorce again a few months ago.
Recently her parents told her to choose: live with Mom or
live with Dad. She got misty-eyed as she described their
announcement. I didn't have a chance to tell her this, but
if I see her again, you can bet your sweet September I am

going to look her square in the eyes and say, "You'll get through this. It won't be painless. It won't be quick. But God will use this mess for good. In the meantime don't be foolish or naive. But don't despair either. Never give up. With God's help you will get through this."

Has it hit you yet that we live in a world of two-hour shipping? Not two days. Not even next day. If you've got an abundance of cash and a dearth of patience, you can click a button and receive your heart's desire in a mere matter of hours.

Oh, how we hate to wait. Oh, how we dread delay.

Alas, our good God offers no express delivery for his great rescue plan. To hope in him is to accept his timing. Patience is not only a virtue—it's a necessity. Each of us must learn to dismiss our demands and hop on heaven's timetable if we want to experience true deliverance.

Is waiting hard? Yes. Is it humbling? Yes. But is it healthy? You bet.

So pump up your patience. Be willing to wait. You'll get through this and be better on the other side. Never give up.

> But those who wait on the LORD
> Shall renew their strength;
> They shall mount up with wings like eagles,

They shall run and not be weary,
They shall walk and not faint. (Isa. 40:31)

Heavenly Father,
I confess my distaste for waiting on you—for waiting on your timing and following your plans. I confess my impatience not just with my circumstances but also with you. According to your great grace and mercy, please teach me how to wait and never give up.

In Jesus' name,
Amen

....

Day 4–God Will Use This Mess for Good
The painter is about to begin her masterpiece when she sees it out of the corner of her eye: a splotch. While prepping her palette, a drop of Cadmium Red must have careened to the floor, making an unsightly blemish on the rosin paper below. "Tsk tsk," she says. A little mineral water on a damp cloth, and the problem is solved. Splotch scrubbed.

She's about to start again—brush poised above the canvass—when she spots another spot. This time it's a little Yellow Ocher on the sleeve of her smock. "Tut tut." That won't do. With a flourish, she removes the smock and glides to the laundry room. Mix a little powdered detergent with warm water to make a paste. Apply. Remove. Apply. Remove. Rinse and scrub. Hang it out to dry for a couple of hours in the sun. Voilà.

By now the light has changed, so she'll have to wait for tomorrow to start her masterpiece once more. Oh well. At least everything is clean.

Does such a scenario make sense at all? No. Of course not. The idea of a painter paralyzed by a little untidiness is laughable. Painters understand that some tasks require a mess. So do auto mechanics. And gourmet chefs.

So does our good God. Like any master craftsman, he's in the business of turning messes into miracles. Even in the most muddled seasons of our lives, he knows exactly how to add a little red here, a little yellow there, adjust the shading with just the smallest amount of gray, and voilà—a blemish becomes a blessing.

When your life feels like a mess, don't throw in the towel. Instead, lean in. Let the Master do his work. Trust that God will use this mess for good. Never give up.

Therefore humble yourselves under the mighty hand of God, that He may exalt you in due time, casting all your care upon Him, for He cares for you. (1 Peter 5:6–7)

Heavenly Father,

It's easy for me to trust you when my life is going well. Please show me how to trust you when my life feels like a mess. I believe you are sovereign. I believe you are in control. Therefore, I choose to trust in your ability to transform a mess into a miracle.

In Jesus' name,

Amen

. . . .

Day 5–Don't Be Foolish or Naive

It might be the silliest moment in all of Scripture. Silly, but serious as well.

Of course it involves Peter. The man must have hopped around Judea on his left foot, because his right was always planted in his mouth.

The whole thing started when Jesus began to talk with the disciples about the future. Specifically, his future. Even more specifically, the cross. "From that time Jesus began to show to His disciples that He must go to Jerusalem, and suffer many things from the elders and chief priests and scribes, and be killed, and be raised the third day" (Matt. 16:21).

The text says ol' Peter took Jesus aside and began to "rebuke" him. Ever seen a mom in a grocery store grab her toddler and yank the poor child down the aisle? "I've told you a hundred times we are *not* going to buy those cookies right now, so you better . . ." That's what Peter did to Jesus. He gave the Teacher a talking-to. He lectured the Lord: "Far be it from You, Lord; this shall not happen to You!" (Matt. 16:22).

Needless to say, the Lord wasn't having it: "But He turned and said to Peter, 'Get behind Me, Satan! You are an offense to Me, for you are not mindful of the things of God, but the things of men'" (v. 23).

Ouch. Peter was foolish. He didn't like Jesus talking about suffering and dying and all that unpleasantness. So he tried to set the record straight by chastising Christ.

Don't be like Peter. Don't dictate to God how he should run the universe. More importantly, don't dictate to God how he should run your life. Or your spouse's life. Or your children's lives.

Instead, be humble. Be receptive. Be submissive to your Savior.

> *Draw near to God and He will draw near to you.*
> *Cleanse your hands, you sinners; and purify your*
> *hearts, you double-minded. . . . Humble yourselves*
> *in the sight of the Lord, and He will lift you up.*
> *(James 4:8–10)*

Heavenly Father,

I know I am like Peter in so many ways. I have so many opinions about how you should fix my problems—and when you should fix my problems. I confess to being foolish and naive. Please fill me with your Spirit and with your wisdom.

In Jesus' name,

Amen

....

Day 6–Don't Despair

Let's get back to Joseph in that pit. That empty cistern. The idea in the ancient world was to dig large holes to collect runoff or rainwater, or sometimes to receive the flow of a diverted stream. These cisterns were often lined with plaster or other materials to prevent leaks. The fact that Joseph's brothers found a "dry cistern" meant that particular example had a leak and had been abandoned as useless, or that the season was too dry for any water to collect.

Either way, you bet your bottom dollar it was a hard hole. An unpleasant landing.

Can you see the scene from Joseph's point of view? The walls of his enclosure shaded in darkness. The opening a glaring circle of sunlight with ten heads looking down. Some of his brothers were grinning like hyenas. Others pulled grim faces—executioner's faces. No word of comfort. No sign this was some kind of practical joke.

You've been there, haven't you? Found yourself suddenly entombed in darkness. Felt the helplessness and fear inhabiting that particular hole. Maybe it was the day divorce papers arrived. Or the visit to your doctor to learn the results of your latest scan. Or the unexpected meeting invite at your boss's office on a Friday afternoon.

Rock bottom.

The next time you land in that terrible spot, grab hold of this treasured truth: You're not alone. Even if it seems like you're alone, even if it feels like you're alone, cling to the knowledge that God is with you, just as he was with Joseph. Right there in the pit. Smack dab in the hole.

Therefore, don't despair. Don't give up. Use every fiber of faith you can muster to grab hold of God's hand and allow him to lead you back into the light.

The righteous cry out, and the Lord hears,
And delivers them out of all their troubles.
The Lord is near to those who have a broken heart,
And saves such as have a contrite spirit. (Ps. 34:17–18)

Heavenly Father,

Chances are good that I will experience a rock-bottom moment sometime in the future. Maybe even sometime soon. Please prepare me. Please surround me. And please help me find you and feel you when that moment comes.

In Jesus' name,

Amen

••••••••••••••••••

Day 7–With God's Help, You'll Get Through This

In more than four decades of ministry, I've met quite a lot of impressive people. Powerful pastors, wonderful writers, amazing administrators, magnificent moms, courageous counselors, laudable leaders, stirring servants, explosive evangelists, and more. I've met people who can fix anything ever built. People who can befriend anyone ever born. And people packed with such jaw-dropping wisdom that I scramble for pen and paper as soon as they start to speak.

Chances are pretty good you make that list as well. You are a unique individual handcrafted by the Creator of the universe. The same God who sparked the stars took on the task of building your brain and planning your personality. Impressive is an understatement when describing you!

Here's the thing: We're often a little too aware of our strengths. Our gifts. Our abilities. More than that, we live in a world where technology claims to accomplish everything from flipping burgers to fusing atoms. We're part of an impressive culture.

It's easy to believe we can handle whatever life throws our way. Cancer schmancer. Laid off schmade off. Depression—uh . . . schmappression? Whatever, I got this.

Or, on the other side of the coin, it's easy to believe we're responsible for handling whatever life throws our way. *You're an adult. Grab those bootstraps and yank yourself forward.*

Nope and nope. Joseph was one of the most impressive people in history, but he couldn't handle his circumstance on his own. He needed God's help. So do I. So do you.

Whatever pit you're at the bottom of right now, you'll get through this. It won't be painless. It won't be quick. But God will use this mess for good. In the meantime, don't despair, but don't be foolish or naive either. Never give up. *With God's help*, you'll get through this.

> *He who dwells in the secret place of the Most High*
> *Shall abide under the shadow of the Almighty.*

Seven Statements of Strength

I will say of the LORD,
"He is my refuge and my fortress;
My God, in Him I will trust." (Ps. 91:1–2)

Heavenly Father,
For my whole life, you've been teaching me about
my limits, but I'm slow to learn. I confess I still try
to handle my problems by myself. Thank you for
your patience, Lord. Thank you for your Spirit.
Please be with me and help me learn to rely on you.

In Jesus' name,

Amen

NOTES

1. Spiros Zodhiates, ed., *The Hebrew-Greek Key Word Study Bible: Key Insights into God's Word, New American Standard Bible*, rev. ed. (Chattanooga, TN: AMG, 2008), Genesis 50:20. See also "Greek/Hebrew Definitions," Bible Tools, Strong's #2803, *chashab*, www.bibletools.org/index.cfm/fuseaction /Lexicon.show/ID/H2803/chashab.htm.
2. Joseph was probably seventeen when he was sold to the Midianites (Gen. 37:2). He was twenty-eight when the butler, who promised to help him get out of prison, was released (40:21–23). Two years later, when Joseph was thirty, Joseph interpreted Pharaoh's dreams (41:1, 46). And Joseph was about thirty-nine when his brothers came to Egypt the second time (45:1–6), in the second year of the famine following the seven years of plenty.
3. "Every shepherd is an abomination to the Egyptians" (Gen. 46:34).

Notes

4. JJ Jasper, personal conversations with the author. Used by permission.

5. Thomas Lye, "How Are We to Live by Faith on Divine Providence?," in *Puritan Sermons, 1659–1689*, ed. James Nichols (Wheaton, IL: Richard Owen Roberts, 1981), 1:378.

6. Edward Mote, "The Solid Rock," in *Sacred Selections for the Church*, comp. and ed. Ellis J. Crum (Kendallville, IN: Sacred Selections, 1960), 120.

7. Augustine, *Saint Augustine: Sermons on the Liturgical Seasons*, trans. Sister Mary Sarah Muldowney (New York: Fathers of the Church, 1959), 85–86.

8. Howard Rutledge and Phyllis Rutledge with Mel White and Lyla White, *In the Presence of Mine Enemies, 1965–1973: A Prisoner of War* (New York: Fleming H. Revell, 1975), 33, 35.

9. Zodhiates, *Hebrew-Greek Key Word Study Bible*, #977, p. 1817. See also *Strong's Concordance with Hebrew and Greek Lexicon*, http://www.eliyah.com/cgi-bin/strongs .cgi?file=hebrewlexicon&isindex=977.

10. Rutledge and Rutledge, *In the Presence*, 39, 52.

11. Psalm 46:10.

12. Joni Eareckson Tada, "God's Plan A," in *Be Still, My Soul: Embracing God's Purpose and Provision in Suffering*, ed. Nancy Guthrie (Wheaton, IL: Crossway, 2010), 32–33, 34.

13. Donald G. Bloesch, *The Struggle of Prayer* (Colorado Springs, CO: Helmers and Howard, 1988), 33.

14. "Spite House," New York Architecture Images, nyc -architecture.com, http://nyc-architecture.com/GON /GON005.htm.

15. *Strong's Exhaustive Bible Concordance Online*, #5117, www.biblestudytools.com/lexicons/greek/nas/topos.html.

16. Rick Reilly, "Matt Steven Can't See the Hoop. But He'll Still Take the Last Shot," Life of Reilly, ESPN.com, March 11, 2009, http://sports.espn.go.com/espnmag/story?id=3967807. See also Gil Spencer, "Blind Player Helps Team See the Value of Sportsmanship," *Delaware County Daily Times*, February 25, 2009, www.delcotimes.com/articles/2009/02/25/sports /doc49a4c50632d09134430615.

17. In retaliation for an attack on their sister, Simeon and Levi slaughtered all the males in the village of Shechem (Gen. 34).

18. "John H. Glenn," National Aeronautics and Space Administration, https://www.nasa.gov/people/john-glenn/.

19. Bob Greene, "John Glenn's True Hero," CNN.com, February 20, 2012, www.cnn.com/2012/02/19/opinion /greene-john-annie-glenn/index.html.

20. From a conversation with Steven Chapman on November 30, 2011. Used by permission.

21. "The Story of Keep Calm and Carry On," YouTube video, 3:01, posted by Temujin Doran, www.youtube.com /watch?v=FrHkKXFRbCI&sns=fb. See also *Keep Calm and Carry On: Good Advice for Hard Times* (Kansas City, MO: Andrews McMeel, 2009), introduction.

Inspired by what you just read?
Connect with Max

UPWORDS

The nonprofit teaching ministry of Max Lucado

Listen to Max's teaching ministry, *UpWords*, on the radio and online.
Visit MaxLucado.com for more resources for spiritual growth
and encouragement, including:

- Archives of *UpWords*, Max's daily radio program,
  and a list of radio stations where it airs
- Daily devotionals and emails from Max
- *The Max Lucado Encouraging Word Podcast*
- *Fresh Hope* YouTube Teaching Show
- Video teaching and articles
- Online store with information on new books and special offers

1-800-822-9673
UpWords Ministries
P.O. Box 692170
San Antonio, TX 78269-2170
info@maxlucado.com

MaxLucado.com

More Encouragement from Max Lucado

The Max Lucado Encouraging Word Podcast is all about the greatest story ever told—the living Savior who brings you a lifetime of hope.

Listen wherever you enjoy podcasts.

Max's YouTube show *FRESH HOPE* features timeless, encouraging teaching. Each episode will shift our focus from our worried, weary world to our good God and the refreshing promises found in his Word.

Watch and subscribe on YouTube.com/MaxLucadoOfficial

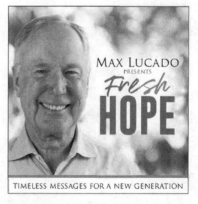

You'll Get Through This.
Whatever "This" Is.

Dive deeper into the story of Joseph with the book and six-session Bible study

MaxLucado.com

.